150 SUPERFOOD RECIPES

A vibrant collection of dishes, packed with powerful, nutrient-rich ingredients, shown in over 500 photographs • AUDREY DEANE

This edition is published by Southwater,
an imprint of Anness Publishing Ltd,
108 Great Russell Street,
London WC1B 3NA
info@anness.com

www.southwaterbooks.com;
www.annesspublishing.com

© Anness Publishing Ltd 2014

PUBLISHER'S NOTE
Although the advice and information
in this book are believed to be
accurate and true at the time of
going to press, neither the authors
nor the publisher can accept any
legal responsibility or liability for any
errors or omissions that may have been
made nor for any inaccuracies or any loss, harm or injury that
comes about from following instructions or advice in this book.

NOTES
Bracketed terms are intended for American readers. For all
recipes, quantities are given in metric and imperial measures and,
where appropriate, in standard cups and spoons. Follow one set
of measures, not a mixture, as they are not interchangeable.

• Standard spoon and cup measures are level. 1 tsp = 5ml, 1
tbsp = 15ml, 1 cup = 250m1/8fl oz. Australian standard
tablespoons are 20ml.
• Australian readers should use 3 tsp in place of I tbsp for
measuring small quantities. American pints are 16fl oz/2 cups.
• American readers should use 20fl oz/2.5 cups in place of 1
pint when measuring liquids.
• Electric oven temperatures in this book are for conventional
ovens. When using a fan oven, the temperature will probably
need to be reduced by about 10–20°C/20–40°F. Since ovens
vary, you should check with your manufacturer's instruction
book for guidance.
• The nutritional analysis given for each recipe is calculated per
portion (i.e. serving or item), unless otherwise stated. If the
recipe gives a range, such as Serves 4–6, then the nutritional
analysis will be for the smaller portion size, i.e. 6 servings.
Measurements for sodium do not include salt added to taste.
Medium (US large) eggs are used unless otherwise stated.

Important: pregnant women, the elderly, the ill and very young
children should avoid recipes using raw or lightly cooked eggs.

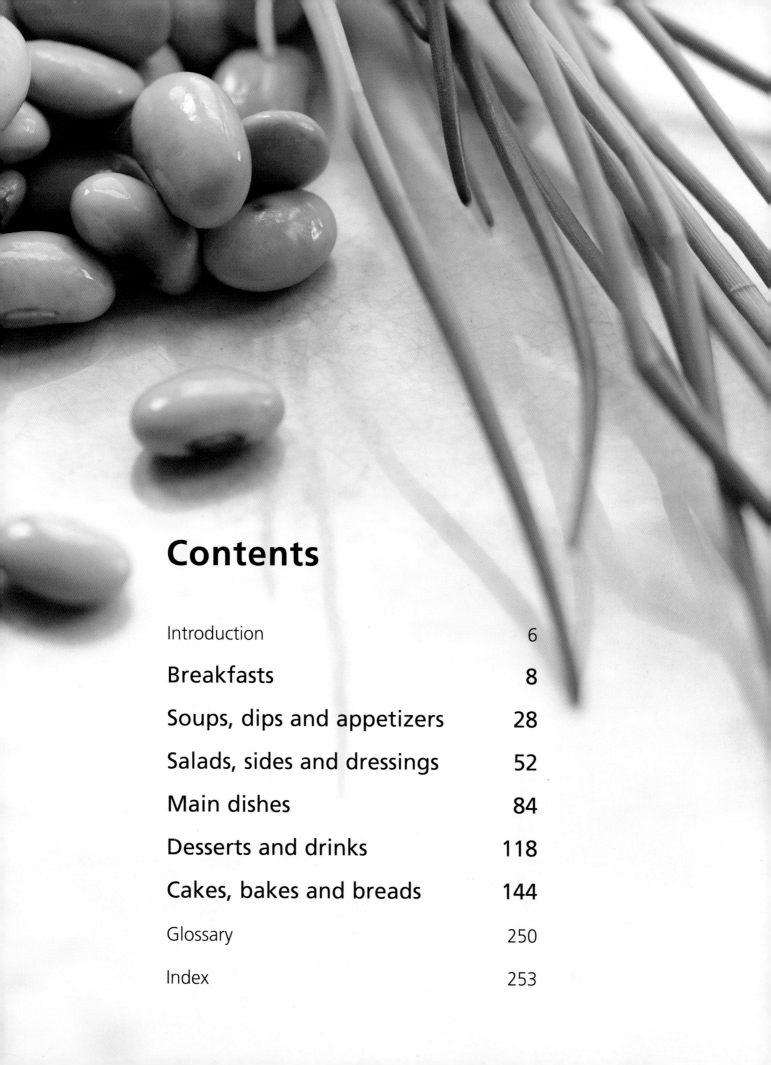

Contents

Introduction

The scientific study of food and its impact on health is well documented and dates back to the 18th century, when learned men and physicians began to travel the world studying the effects of nutritional deficiencies. One of the best-known breakthroughs was the realization that citrus fruits could prevent scurvy among sailors. However, it was not until the late 1920s, with the discovery of vitamin C, that people fully understood what it was in the citrus fruits that kept the disease at bay. By this time the number of researchers working in the field of nutritional science had exploded, and this 'Golden Age' of nutritional analysis led to the discovery of many of the basic factors required to maintain a healthy diet.

This research has continued into the modern day and, with more sophisticated scientific procedures, new findings are being made all the time, although the claims of some supposed 'superfoods' have not stood up to modern scientific scrutiny. It is worth noting that, although widely used, the word 'superfood' is not legally recognized , but it is used to describe foods with a high nutritional content.

Below: Orange juice is a quick and easy source of vitamin C.

FOOD FOR HEALTH
There are a wide range of highly nutritious substances found in foods, sometimes termed phytonutrients, or phytochemicals, that are reported to have beneficial effects on health and well-being.

Foods High in Antioxidants
Antioxidant-rich foods, such as blueberries, goji berries, oranges and tomatoes, are usually part of the fruit and vegetable family. Antioxidants are thought to be crucial for our well being due to their powerful ability to 'mop up' free radicals that circulate around the body. Many vitamins have antioxidant activity, such as vitamin A (retinol), vitamin C (ascorbic acid) and vitamin E (tocopherol) as well as some minerals, including selenium. All have a vital role to play in keeping potentially harmful substances in check and preventing them from causing diseases such as cancer.

Foods High in Flavonoids
Also known as polyphenols, flavonoids are found in tea and red wine and in chocolate. Flavonoids have some antioxidant activity, but it is their role in cell signalling that is the basis for their reported health benefits. Studies have shown that they are able to regulate the cell signals and can affect cell growth, thus possibly influencing cancer incidence. These compounds could also reduce the risk of coronary heart disease and atherosclerosis and may also have beneficial effects in brain disorders such as Alzheimer's and Parkinson's disease.

Foods High in Phytosterols
These important compounds, found in wheatgerm and brown rice, may have the ability to lower blood cholesterol levels by altering the way it is metabolized by the body. Found in plant cells, phytosterols are the plant equivalent of animal cholesterol.

Above: Antioxidant-rich berries may help to counteract acid-free radicals.

Foods High in Isoflavones and Phytoestrogens
These substances, present in foods such as soya beans, alfalfa and chickpeas, show strong antioxidant activity and also provide dietary oestrogens that have beneficial effects on some of the hormonal systems of the body. These include helping to control blood cholesterol and reducing negative effects of the menopause such as osteoporosis.

Foods High in Dietary Fibre
Fibre can help improve your gastrointestinal health and glucose metabolism, helping those suffering from Type II Diabetes. It can help reduce coronary heart disease risk factors by reducing bad blood fats and hypertension, and also reduce the risk of developing some cancers.

Foods High in Healthy Fats
We now recognize that though many of us would benefit from lower-fat diets, the type of fats we are consuming is equally important. Generally, we should be eating fewer saturated varieties and more of the healthy fats – mono-unsaturated and polyunsaturated fat. These healthy

fats, present in foods such as olive oil, oily fish, flaxseed and walnuts, are important as they influence how we control cholesterol in our bodies.

Healthy omega-3 fats (part of the polyunsaturated fat family) are particularly important as they have many unique roles to play in the body, ranging from brain structure and function to potentially reducing excessive inflammatory reactions such as rheumatoid arthritis.

SUPERFOODS
There is a wide range of foods that are thought to provide particularly high levels of nutrients.

Fruit and Vegetables
Best eaten raw to gain maximum benefit, every type of fruit is an excellent source of energy and provides valuable fibre and antioxidants, which are said to reduce the risk of heart disease and certain cancers. Vegetables are another essential component of a healthy diet and have countless nutritional benefits, especially when freshly picked.

Cereal Grains
The seeds of cereal grasses are packed with concentrated goodness and are an important source of complex starchy carbohydrates, protein, vitamins and minerals. When eaten as wholegrains they offer us the most health benefits.

Legumes and Pulses
Lentils and beans provide the cook with a diverse range of flavours and textures. Low in fat and high in complex carbohydrates, vitamins and minerals, the phytonutrient content of legumes is varied and the combined effect of this makes them a very valuable food to us.

Nuts and Seeds
The storage fruits of trees, nuts are full of nutrients and oils, particularly in B vitamins, vitamin E, potassium,

Above: For optimum nutrition eat wholegrain carbohydrates.

magnesium, calcium, phosphorus and iron. Nuts are also a good source of fibre and phytosterols, and most contain mainly unsaturated fat. There is mounting evidence that eating nuts regularly contributes to a reduced risk of cardiovascular disease. Similarly, seeds are nutritional powerhouses, packed with vitamins and minerals, as well as beneficial oils and protein.

Spices and Oils
Still prized for their reputed medicinal properties and culinary uses, spices play a vital role in creating healthy and appetizing cooking. Their health benefits are often attributed to the intense aromatic, volatile oils they contain. Oils that are rich in monounsaturated fat, such as olive oil, have been found to reduce 'bad' LDL cholesterol, and its polyphenol content exerts some anti-inflammatory effects as well as keeping blood vessels elastic.

Dairy Produce
Eaten in moderation, dairy products provide valuable nutrients such as calcium, which is in its most bioavailable form, vitamin B_{12} and vitamins A and D. Dairy products do provide a complete protein source for vegetarians, and if lower fat options are selected can be consumed as part of a very healthy balanced diet.

Animal Protein
Meat and poultry provide valuable, high-quality proteins full of essential amino acids that our bodies cannot make. It also contains the most bioavailable form of iron, as well as zinc and magnesium. Meat and poultry contain a wide array of B-vitamins, including vitamin B_{12}, which is not found in plant-based foods. Fish and seafood can be split into three groups: white fish, oily fish and seafood. White fish is an excellent low-fat source of protein and is easy to digest. Oily fish is slightly higher in fat, but it is a 'good' fat, called omega-3, which we all need to eat more of because of the potential benefits, such as brain and eye development and maintenance, and heart health. Seafood is also rich in omega-3 fats and is a great source of protein as well.

THE RECIPES IN THIS BOOK
All of the superfoods used in the following recipes can make valuable contributions to health, especially when a wide variety are introduced. The recipes are split into chapters to make it easy to plan a week of healthy meals, for maximum nutrient-packed, energizing, detoxifying and immunity-strengthening impact.

Below: Oily fish, such as mackerel, is full of essential amino acids.

Essential minerals and vitamins

Regular intake of a wide range of minerals and vitamins is essential for good health, and the vast majority can be found in many different foods. By frequently eating enough of the correct foods, including at least five portions of fruit and vegetables per day, most people should not need to take vitamin or mineral supplements. An exception to this is vitamin B12, which is only found in animal products and yeast extracts, so if you are vegan you may need to take this in supplement form. Try to eat a variety of different types and colours of produce each day, in particular brightly coloured and dark green fruit and vegetables, to ensure that you are obtaining as wide a range of nutrients and beneficial compounds as possible. This chart describes which foods are the richest sources, the role the mineral or vitamin plays in health maintenance, and the signs that may suggest a deficiency.

MINERAL	BEST SOURCES	ROLE IN HEALTH	DEFICIENCY
Calcium	Canned sardines (with bones), dairy products, green leafy vegetables, sesame seeds, dried figs and almonds.	Essential for building and maintaining strong bones and teeth, muscle function and the nervous system.	Deficiency is characterized by soft and brittle bones, osteoporosis, fractures and muscle weakness.
Chloride	Nuts, wholegrains, beans, peas, lentils, tofu and black tea.	Regulates and maintains the balance of fluids in the body.	Deficiency is rare.
Iodine	Seafood, seaweed and iodized salt.	Aids the production of hormones released by the thyroid gland.	Deficiency can lead to sluggish metabolism, and dry skin and hair.
Iron	Meat, offal, sardines, egg yolks, fortified cereals, leafy vegetables, dried apricots, tofu and cocoa.	Essential for healthy blood and muscles.	Deficiency is characterized by anaemia, fatigue and low resistance to infection.
Magnesium	Nuts, seeds, wholegrains, beans, peas, lentils, tofu, dried figs and apricots, and green vegetables.	Essential for healthy muscles, bones and teeth, normal growth, and nerves.	Deficiency is characterized by lethargy, weak bones and muscles, depression and irritability.
Manganese	Nuts, wholegrains, beans, lentils, brown rice, tofu and black tea.	Essential component of enzymes involved in energy production.	Deficiency is not characterized by any specific symptoms.
Phosphorus	Found in most foods, especially lean meat, poultry, fish, eggs, dairy products and nuts.	Essential for healthy bones and teeth, energy production and the absorption of many nutrients.	Deficiency is rare.
Potassium	Bananas, milk, beans, peas, lentils, nuts, seeds, whole grains, potatoes, fruit and vegetables.	Essential for water balance, regulating blood pressure, and nerve transmission.	Deficiency is characterized by weakness, thirst, fatigue, mental confusion and raised blood pressure.
Selenium	Meat, fish, citrus fruits, avocados, lentils, milk, cheese, Brazil nuts and seaweed.	Essential for protecting against free radical damage and may protect against cancer – an antioxidant.	Deficiency is characterized by reduced antioxidant protection.
Sodium	Found in most foods, but comes mainly from processed foods.	Essential for nerve and muscle function and body fluid regulation.	Deficiency is unlikely but can lead to dehydration and cramps.
Zinc	Lean meat, oysters, peanuts, cheese, wholegrains, seeds, beans, peas and lentils.	Essential for a healthy immune system, normal growth, wound healing, and reproduction.	Deficiency is characterized by impaired growth, slow wound healing, and loss of taste and smell.

VITAMIN	BEST SOURCES	ROLE IN HEALTH	DEFICIENCY
A (retinol in animal foods, betacarotene in plant foods)	Animal sources: liver, oily fish, milk, butter, cheese, egg yolks and margarine. Plant sources: orange-fleshed and dark green fruit and vegetables.	Essential for vision, bone growth, and skin and tissue repair. Beta-carotene acts as an antioxidant and protects the immune system.	Deficiency is characterized by poor night vision, dry skin and lower resistance to infection, especially respiratory disorders.
B1 (thiamin)	Lean meat (especially pork), wholegrain and fortified bread and cereals, brewer's yeast, potatoes, nuts, beans, peas, lentils and milk.	Essential for energy production, the nervous system, muscles, and heart. Promotes growth and boosts mental ability.	Deficiency is characterized by depression, irritability, nervous disorders, loss of memory. Common among alcoholics.
B2 (riboflavin)	Meat (especially liver), dairy, eggs, fortified bread and cereals, yeast extract and almonds.	Essential for energy production and for the functioning of vitamin B6 and niacin, as well as tissue repair.	Deficiency is characterized by lack of energy, dry cracked lips, numbness and itchy eyes.
Niacin (nicotinic acid, also called B3)	Lean meat, fish, beans, peas, lentils, potatoes, fortified breakfast cereals, wheatgerm, nuts, milk, eggs, peas, mushrooms, green leafy vegetables, figs and prunes.	Essential for healthy digestive system, skin and circulation. It is also needed for the release of energy.	Deficiency is unusual, but characterized by lack of energy, depression and scaly skin.
B6 (piridoxine)	Lean meat, fish, eggs, wholegrain cereals, brown rice, nuts and cruciferous vegetables, such as broccoli, cabbage and cauliflower.	Essential for assimilating protein and fat, for making red blood cells, and maintaining a healthy immune system.	Deficiency is characterized by anaemia, dermatitis and depression.
B12 (cyano-cobalamin)	Meat (especially liver), fish, milk, eggs, fortified breakfast cereals, cheese and yeast extract.	Essential for growth, formation of red blood cells and maintaining a healthy nervous system.	Deficiency is characterized by fatigue, increased risk of infection, and anaemia.
Folate (folic acid)	Offal, dark green leafy vegetables, wholegrain and fortified breakfast cereals, bread, nuts, beans, peas, lentils, bananas and yeast extract.	Essential for cell division; especially needed before conception and during pregnancy.	Deficiency is characterized by anaemia and appetite loss. Linked with neural defects in babies.
C (ascorbic acid)	Citrus fruit, melons, strawberries, tomatoes, broccoli, potatoes, (bell) peppers and green vegetables.	Essential for the absorption of iron, healthy skin, teeth and bones. Strengthens the immune system and helps to fight infection.	Deficiency is characterized by increased susceptibility to infection, fatigue, poor sleep and depression.
D (calciferol)	Mainly exposure to sunlight. Also liver, oily fish, eggs, fortified breakfast cereals and fortified dairy produce.	Essential for bone and tooth formation; helps the body to absorb calcium and phosphorus.	Deficiency is characterized by softening of the bones, muscle weakness and anaemia. Shortage in children can cause rickets.
E (tocopherols)	Oily fish, seeds, nuts, vegetable oils, eggs, wholemeal bread, avocados and spinach.	Essential for healthy skin, circulation, and maintaining cells – an antioxidant.	Deficiency is characterized by increased risk of heart attack, strokes and certain cancers.

BREAKFAST

Breakfast, the most important meal of the day, is about fuelling your body to get going after the night's fast – everyone needs something, no matter how hectic a lifestyle they lead. There are plenty of alternatives to shop-bought sugary cereals and fatty fry-ups, and this chapter is packed with ideas for everyday healthy morning meals, from quick on-the-move smoothies and breakfast bars to more indulgent weekend specials, such as Lentil Kitchiri or Smoked Salmon with Scrambled Eggs.

Raspberry and oatmeal blend

This delightful combination of juicy, tangy raspberries with creamy bio-yogurt and oatmeal will see you right through to lunch with its slow-release energy. Using fresh raspberries, this drink ensures that the benefits of the antioxidants, anthocyanins and flavonoids are retained.

Serves 1

25ml/1½ tbsp medium oatmeal
150g/5oz/scant 1 cup raspberries
5–10ml/1–2 tsp clear honey
45ml/3 tbsp low-fat bio-yogurt

1 Put the oatmeal into a heatproof bowl. Pour in 120ml/4fl oz/½ cup boiling water and leave to stand for about 10 minutes or until the water has been completely absorbed.

2 Put the soaked oats in a blender or food processor and add all but two or three of the raspberries, the honey and about 30ml/2 tbsp of the yogurt. Purée until smooth, scraping the mix down from the sides if necessary.

3 Pour the smoothie into a large glass, swirl in the remaining yogurt and top with raspberries. Chill in the refrigerator – it will thicken up, so you might need to add a little juice or mineral water before serving.

> **SUPERFOOD TIP**
> The live bacteria present within bio-yogurt aid digestion.

Frozen berry and chlorella smoothie

This smoothie is packed full of berries and is a perfect pick-me-up on a hot day. This refreshing drink is positively bursting with lots of supernutrient goodness. The crushed ice makes this a revitalizing beverage that is lighter than many other smoothie drinks.

Serves 1

10 ice cubes
150g/5oz/scant 1 cup mixed
   berries (raspberries, blackberries,
   redcurrants and blackcurrants)
60ml/4 tbsp cranberry juice
10ml/2 tsp chlorella powder

1 Place all of the ice cubes in a freezer bag and use a rolling pin to crush them, then set aside.

2 Put the berries in a food processor or blender and add the cranberry juice. Pulse until the mixture breaks down into a thick purée.

3 Add the chlorella powder to the food processor or blender and pulse again until it is mixed into the purée. Finally, add the crushed ice and blend well. Pour the smoothie into a large glass and serve while it still chilled.

Raspberry and oatmeal blend: Energy 186Kcal/793kJ; Protein 7.5g; Carbohydrate 34.6g, of which sugars 16.4g; Fat 3.1g, of which saturates 0.4g; Cholesterol 1mg; Calcium 137mg; Fibre 5.5g; Sodium 51mg.
Frozen berry and chlorella smoothie: Energy 37Kcal/161kJ; Protein 2g; Carbohydrate 8g, of which sugars 8g; Fat 0g, of which saturates 0g; Cholesterol 0mg; Calcium 70mg; Fibre 5.3g; Sodium 22mg.

Wheat bran smoothie

This high-fibre, fruity smoothie makes a great start to the day. Wheat bran and bananas provide slow-release carbohydrate to keep your energy levels stable, while fresh orange juice and sweet, fragrant mango will provide a fantastic boost to your vitamin and mineral requirements.

Serves 2

½ mango
1 banana
1 large orange
30ml/2 tbsp wheat bran
15ml/1 tbsp sesame seeds
10–15ml/2 tsp–1 tbsp honey

COOK'S TIP
Mango juice is naturally very sweet so you may wish to add less honey or leave it out altogether. Taste the drink to decide how much you need.

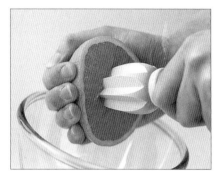

1 Using a small, sharp knife, skin the mango, then slice the flesh off the stone (pit). Peel the banana and break it into short lengths, then place it in a blender or food processor together with the skinned mango.

2 Squeeze the juice from the orange and add to the blender or food processor along with the bran, sesame seeds and honey. Whizz until the mixture is smooth and creamy, then pour into glasses and serve.

Wheat bran smoothie: Energy 172kcal/726kJ; Protein 4.9g; Carbohydrate 27.6g, of which sugars 23.1g; Fat 5.5g, of which saturates 0.9g; Cholesterol 0mg; Calcium 102mg; Fibre 8.5g; Sodium 11mg.

Wheatgrass tonic

Wheatgrass is grown from wheat seeds and is a concentrated source of chlorophyll and the antioxidant vitamins A, C and E. It does have a distinctive, sweet flavour so this juice is blended with mild white cabbage, but it is just as tasty combined with other vegetables or fruit juices instead.

Serves 1

50g/2oz white cabbage
90g/3½oz wheatgrass

1 Cut the core from the cabbage and roughly shred the leaves. Push through a juicer with the wheatgrass (a masticating juicer is best).

2 Pour the juice into a small glass and serve immediately.

Pineapple and ginger juice

Fresh root ginger is one of the best natural cures for stomach cramps and nausea. In this unusual fruity blend, it is simply mixed with fresh, juicy pineapple and sweet-tasting carrot, creating a quick and easy remedy that can be juiced in minutes – and which tastes delicious too.

Serves 1

½ small pineapple
25g/1oz fresh root ginger
1 carrot
ice cubes

1 Using a sharp knife, cut away the skin from the pineapple, then halve and remove the core. Roughly slice the pineapple flesh. Peel and roughly chop the ginger, then chop the carrot.

2 Push the carrot, ginger and pineapple through a juicer and pour into a glass. Add ice cubes and serve immediately.

COOK'S TIP
Before preparing the pineapple, leave it upside down for 30 minutes – this makes it juicier.

Wheatgrass tonic: Energy 36kcal/149kJ; Protein 3.2g; Carbohydrate 3.9g, of which sugars 3.8g; Fat 0.8g, of which saturates 0.1g; Cholesterol 0mg; Calcium 178mg; Fibre 2.9g; Sodium 130mg.
Pineapple and ginger juice: Energy 120Kcal/516kJ; Protein 1.1g; Carbohydrate 30.2g, of which sugars 29.9g; Fat 0.4g, of which saturates 0.1g; Cholesterol 0mg; Calcium 33mg; Fibre 1.2g; Sodium 33mg.

Dried fruit salad

Inspired by a traditional Scandinavian dessert dish, this recipe uses a wonderful array of dried fruits. Concentrated versions of their fresh counterparts, dried fruits are a rich source of vitamins, minerals and fibre, and will also count as one of the five recommended daily portions of fruit and vegetables.

Serves 6–8

50g/2oz/¼ cup currants
50g/2oz/¼ cup sultanas (golden raisins)
115g/4oz/½ cup dried apricots
115g/4oz/½ cup prunes
115g/4oz/½ cup dried apples
115g/4oz/½ cup dried peaches
115g/4oz/½ cup dried pears
15ml/1 tbsp lemon zest
7.5cm/3in cinnamon stick
5 whole cloves
40g/1½oz/¼ cup quick-cook tapioca
250ml/8fl oz/1 cup thick, creamy natural (plain) bio-yogurt

1 Chop all the dried fruit and place in a large pan together with 1 litre/1¾ pints/4 cups water. Cover, and leave to stand for at least 2 hours or overnight.

2 Stir the lemon zest, cinnamon stick, cloves and tapioca into the dried fruit mixture. Bring to the boil, cover and simmer for 1 hour, stirring occasionally.

3 Remove the pan from the heat. Take out the cinnamon stick and discard. Allow the fruit mixture to cool slightly before serving.

4 Serve the warm fruit salad topped with a generous dollop of thick and creamy bio-yogurt. You can refrigerate any leftover fruit for up to three days.

Dried fruit salad: Energy 305kcal/1277kJ; Protein 2.7g; Carbohydrate 37.4g, of which sugars 31.5g; Fat 17.1g, of which saturates 10.4g; Cholesterol 43mg; Calcium 51mg; Fibre 4g; Sodium 17mg.

Minted pomegranate yogurt and grapefruit

In this Moroccan-inspired dish, the ruby-red pomegranate seeds add texture, flavour and colour to the yogurt as well as a healthy-heart boost with their polyphenol content. The delicately scented grapefruit salad adds a zesty, refreshing zing to this delicious recipe.

Serves 4

300ml/½ pint/1¼ cups Greek
   (US strained plain) yogurt
2–3 ripe pomegranates
bunch of mint, finely chopped
honey or sugar, to taste (optional)

For the grapefruit salad
2 red grapefruits
2 pink grapefruits
1 white grapefruit
15–30ml/1–2 tbsp orange
   flower water
handful of pomegranate seeds
   and mint leaves, to decorate

1 Put the yogurt in a bowl and beat well. Cut open the pomegranates and scoop out the seeds, removing all the bitter pith. Fold the pomegranate seeds and chopped mint into the yogurt. Sweeten with a little honey or sugar, if using, then chill until ready to serve.

2 Peel the red, pink and white grapefruits, cutting off all the pith. Cut between the membranes to remove the segments, holding the fruit over a bowl to catch the juices.

3 Discard the membranes and mix the fruit segments with the reserved juices. Sprinkle with the orange flower water and add a little honey or sugar, if using. Stir gently.

4 Decorate the chilled yogurt with a scattering of pomegranate seeds and mint leaves, and serve with the grapefruit salad.

COOK'S TIP
Immerse pomegranates in a bowl of water when removing the seeds to help separate the bitter pith.

Minted pomegranate yogurt: Energy 188Kcal/784kJ; Protein 8.8g; Carbohydrate 18g, of which sugars 18g; Fat 10.5g of which saturates 5.2g; Cholesterol 0mg; Calcium 202mg; Fibre 3.6g; Sodium 82mg.

Raspberry cranachan

Bio-yogurt is substituted in for the double (heavy) cream in this traditional Scottish dessert recipe, making it a tempting but lighter breakfast option. Fresh antioxidant-rich raspberries and heart-healthy oats add the superfood elements that will help you to kick-start your day.

Serves 4

75g/3oz crunchy oat cereal
600ml/1 pint/2½ cups thick,
   creamy natural (plain)
   bio-yogurt
250g/9oz/1⅓ cups raspberries
heather honey, to serve

1 Preheat the grill (broiler) to high. Spread the oat cereal on a baking sheet and place under the hot grill for 3–4 minutes, stirring regularly. Set aside on a plate to cool.

2 When the cereal has cooled completely, fold it into the bio-yogurt.

3 Gently fold in 200g/7oz/generous 1 cup of the raspberries, being careful not to crush them.

4 Spoon the creamy mixture into four serving glasses or dishes, and top with the remaining raspberries.

5 Serve the crunchy raspberry cranachan immediately. Pass around a dish of heather honey to drizzle over the top, adding extra sweetness and flavour to this irresistible breakfast dish.

VARIATION
You can use almost any berries for this recipe. Stawberries and blackberries work very well. If you choose strawberries, remove the stalks and cut them into quarters beforehand.

Raspberry cranachan: Energy 276kcal/1152kJ; Protein 12.4g; Carbohydrate 17.2g, of which sugars 11.1g; Fat 19.7g, of which saturates 8.7g; Cholesterol 0mg; Calcium 255mg; Fibre 2.5g; Sodium 122mg.

Amaranth and honey porridge

The sweetness of the honey complements the slightly nutty flavour of the highly nutritious amaranth grain. The relatively heavy texture of the porridge can be lightened with the addition of your favourite fruit, dried or fresh and has the added benefit of being gluten-free.

Serves 1

100g/3¾oz amaranth grain
200ml/7fl oz milk
1 tsp honey

1 Place the milk, amaranth and honey in a pan. Heat gently, stirring occasionally for 15 minutes.

2 When the mixture becomes a porridge-like consistency, pour into a bowl and serve warm.

Popped amaranth cereal

This interesting cooking method follows a tradition of popping cereals such as rice or wheat. High in protein, B-vitamins and minerals, this grain is a nutrient-packed way to start the day. You can add some to your usual cereal or use as a delicious topping for fruit or yogurt.

Serves 1

20g/¾oz amaranth grain
2.5ml/½ tsp ground cinnamon
2.5ml/½ tsp runny honey

1 Heat a heavy-bottomed pan, with the lid on.

2 Place half the amaranth grain in the pan and shake to form a thin layer of grains. The popping should start immediately.

3 Gently shake the pan to ensure even distribution of heat so that the grains do not burn.

4 When the popping has stopped, after about 30 seconds, remove the pan from the heat and pour the popped amaranth into a bowl.

5 Repeat with the other half of the grain and add to the bowl. Add the cinnamon and honey to the popped grain and mix well.

Amaranth and honey porridge: Energy 486Kcal/2042kJ; Protein 21g; Carbohydrate 81g, of which sugars 17g; Fat 10g, of which saturates 3g; Cholesterol 12mg; Calcium 242mg; Fibre 6.7g; Sodium 91mg.
Popped amaranth cereal: Energy 86Kcal/360kJ; Protein 3g; Carbohydrate 16g, of which sugars 3g; Fat 1g, of which saturates 0g; Cholesterol 0mg; Calcium 13mg; Fibre 1.3g; Sodium 2mg.

Porridge with dates and pistachio nuts

A bowl of heart-warming porridge on a cold winter's morning is so comforting, and it is good to know that it's helping your heart stay healthy too. Oats are an excellent way to help reduce bad cholesterol in our bodies and, as they release energy slowly, should stop you snacking mid-morning.

Serves 4

250g/9oz/scant 2 cups fresh dates
225g/8oz/2 cups rolled oats
475ml/16fl oz/2 cups milk
pinch of salt (optional)
50g/2oz/½ cup shelled, unsalted
   pistachio nuts, roughly chopped

SUPERFOOD TIP

Oats have a reputation for being warming foods due to their fat and protein content, which is greater than that of most other grains. As well as providing sustained energy levels, oats are also one of the most nutritious cereals available.

---

1 First make the date purée. Halve the dates and remove the stones (pits) and stems. Cover the halved dates with boiling water and soak for 30 minutes, until softened. Strain, reserving 90ml/6 tbsp of the soaking water.

2 Remove the skin from the dates and purée them in a food processor with the reserved soaking water.

3 Place the oats in a pan with the milk, 300ml/½ pint/1¼ cups water and salt. Bring the porridge to the boil, then reduce the heat and simmer for 4–5 minutes until cooked, stirring frequently.

4 Serve the porridge in warm serving bowls, topped with a spoonful of the date purée and sprinkled with chopped pistachio nuts.

Porridge with dates: Energy 416Kcal/1754kJ; Protein 13.6g; Carbohydrate 62.5g, of which sugars 21.2g; Fat 13.8g, of which saturates 1.3g; Cholesterol 0mg; Calcium 75mg; Fibre 5.7g; Sodium 127mg.

Apricot bran muffins

These moist, fruity muffins are a nutritious option for breakfast. Apricots are packed with iron, fibre and vitamin A and their calcium content is further boosted by the yogurt and milk in the recipe. The apricots and bran mean that these are high in fibre too.

4 In a large bowl, mix together the flour, bran, bicarbonate of soda, sugar and chopped apricots.

5 Add the melted butter, yogurt and milk to the bowl of dry ingredients. Mix lightly.

6 Two-thirds fill the prepared paper cases with batter. Bake for 15–20 minutes, until a skewer inserted into the centre of one comes out clean.

7 Leave to set for 5 minutes, then turn out on to a wire rack to cool. Serve warm or eat within 2 days.

Makes 12

115g/4oz/1 cup dried apricots
225g/8oz/2 cups self-raising
   (self-rising) flour
50g/2oz/½ cup wheat or
   oat bran
2.5ml/½ tsp bicarbonate of soda
   (baking soda)
30ml/2 tbsp soft light brown sugar
30ml/2 tbsp butter, melted
150g/5oz/⅔ cup natural
   (plain) yogurt
200ml/7fl oz/scant 1 cup milk

1 Grease the cups of a muffin tin (pan) or line them with paper cases.

2 Soak the dried apricots in a small bowl of water for 15 minutes. Roughly chop the soaked apricots into small bitesize pieces.

3 Preheat the oven to 220°C/425°F/ Gas 7.

> **SUPERFOOD TIP**
> Dried apricots have an even higher concentration of beta-carotene than fresh ones. This powerful antioxidant is believed to lower the risk of cataracts, heart disease and some forms of cancer.

Apricot bran muffins: Energy 131kcal/553kJ; Protein 4g; Carbohydrate 23.6g, of which sugars 8.3g; Fat 3g, of which saturates 1.7g; Cholesterol 7mg; Calcium 83mg; Fibre 2.7g; Sodium 42mg.

Cranberry, apple and walnut muffins

Sweet, sharp and decidedly moreish, these muffins are richly spiced and packed with plenty of fruity flavours. Apples and cranberries both contain polyphenols, which may be beneficial in helping to reduce the risk of cancer and cardiovascular disease.

Makes 12

1 egg
50g/2oz/¼ cup butter, melted
100g/3¾oz/generous ½ cup caster (superfine) sugar
grated rind of 1 large orange
120ml/4fl oz/½ cup freshly squeezed orange juice
140g/5oz/1¼ cups plain (all-purpose) flour
5ml/1 tsp baking powder
2.5ml/½ tsp ground cinnamon
2.5ml/½ tsp freshly grated nutmeg
2.5ml/½ tsp ground allspice
pinch of ground ginger
pinch of salt
2 small eating apples
170g/6oz/1½ cups fresh cranberries
55g/2oz/1⅓ cups walnuts, chopped

1 Preheat the oven to 180°C/350°F/Gas 4. Lightly grease the cups of a muffin tin (pan) or line them with paper cases.

2 In a bowl, whisk the egg with the melted butter to combine. Add the sugar, grated orange rind and juice. Whisk to blend. Set aside.

3 In a large bowl, sift together the flour, baking powder, cinnamon, nutmeg, allspice, ginger and salt.

4 Make a well in the dry ingredients and pour in the egg mixture. With a spoon, stir until just blended.

5 Peel, core and quarter the apples. Chop the apple flesh coarsely with a sharp knife.

6 Add the apples, cranberries and walnuts to the batter and stir lightly to blend.

7 Three-quarters fill the cups. Bake for 25–30 minutes, until golden. Leave to stand for 5 minutes before transferring to a wire rack and allowing to cool. Store in an airtight container for up to 3 days.

Cranberry and apple muffins: Energy 149kcal/624kJ; Protein 2.5g; Carbohydrate 20.4g, of which sugars 10.8g; Fat 6.9g, of which saturates 2.6g; Cholesterol 25mg; Calcium 30mg; Fibre 0.9g; Sodium 34mg.

Fruit and coconut breakfast bars

A perfect breakfast solution when time is short. Instead of buying cereal bars from the supermarket, try making this quick and easy version. Along with the positive effects of coconut on body fat, not skipping breakfast is a good way to get the metabolism going in the morning.

Makes 12

270g/10oz jar apple sauce
115g/4oz/½ cup ready-to-eat dried
  apricots, chopped
115g/4oz/¾ cup raisins
50g/2oz/¼ cup demerara (raw)
  sugar
50g/2oz/⅓ cup sunflower seeds
25g/1oz/2 tbsp sesame seeds
25g/1oz/¼ cup pumpkin seeds
75g/3oz/scant 1 cup rolled oats
75g/3oz/⅔ cup self-raising
  (self-rising) wholemeal (whole-
  wheat) flour
50g/2oz/⅔ cup desiccated (dry
  unsweetened shredded) coconut
2 eggs, beaten

1 Preheat the oven to 200°C/400°F/ Gas 6. Grease a 20cm/8in square shallow baking tin (pan) and line with baking parchment.

2 Pour the apple sauce into a large bowl, then add the apricots, raisins, sugar, and the sunflower, sesame and pumpkin seeds. Stir together with a wooden spoon until thoroughly mixed.

3 Add the oats, flour, coconut and eggs to the fruit mixture and gently stir together until evenly combined.

4 Turn the mixture into the tin and spread to the edges in an even layer. Bake for about 25 minutes, or until golden and just firm to the touch.

5 Leave to cool in the tin, then lift out on to a board and cut into bars.

Fruit and coconut breakfast bars: Energy 207kcal/871kJ; Protein 4.9g; Carbohydrate 29.6g, of which sugars 19.3g; Fat 8.5g, of which saturates 3g; Cholesterol 32mg; Calcium 67mg; Fibre 2.8g; Sodium 46mg.

Lentil kitchiri

This spicy lentil and rice dish is a delicious vegetarian variation of kedgeree. Served with quartered hard-boiled eggs, it is a tasty, high-protein breakfast that is rich in iron. This is a perfect recipe for vegetarians in particular, whose diets can often be low in iron.

Serves 4

50g/2oz/¼ cup dried red
   lentils, rinsed
1 bay leaf
225g/8oz/1 cup basmati rice,
   rinsed
4 cloves
30ml//2 tbsp vegetable oil
5ml/1 tsp curry powder
2.5ml/½ tsp mild chilli powder
30ml/2 tbsp chopped flat
   leaf parsley
salt and ground black pepper
4 hard-boiled eggs, quartered,
   to serve (optional)

1 Put the lentils in a pan, add the bay leaf and cover with cold water. Bring to the boil, skim off any foam, then reduce the heat. Cover and simmer for 25–30 minutes, until the lentils are tender. Drain, then discard the bay leaf.

2 Meanwhile, place the rice in a pan and cover with 475ml/16fl oz/2 cups boiling water. Add the cloves and a generous pinch of salt. Cook, covered, for 10–15 minutes, until all the water is absorbed and the rice is tender. Discard the cloves.

3 Heat the oil in a large frying pan over a gentle heat. Add the curry and chilli powders and cook for 1 minute.

4 Stir in the lentils and rice and mix well until they are coated in the spiced oil. Season and cook for 1–2 minutes, until heated through. Stir in the parsley and serve with the hard-boiled eggs, if using.

Lentil kitchiri: Energy 339kcal/1414kJ; Protein 7.6g; Carbohydrate 52.4g, of which sugars 0.7g; Fat 10.9g, of which saturates 6.5g; Cholesterol 27mg; Calcium 44mg; Fibre 1.3g; Sodium 85mg.

Frittata with sun-dried tomatoes

This Italian omelette, made with tangy Parmesan cheese, can be served warm or cold. The rich, intense flavour of the sun-dried tomatoes and the aromatic thyme really livens up this egg dish. The tomatoes contain lycopene, a powerful antioxidant that could help prevent prostate cancer.

Serves 4

6 sun-dried tomatoes
30ml/2 tbsp olive oil
1 small onion, finely chopped
pinch of fresh thyme leaves
6 eggs
25g/1oz/⅓ cup freshly grated
   Parmesan cheese, plus shavings
   to serve
salt and ground black pepper
thyme sprigs, to garnish

1 Place the sun-dried tomatoes in a bowl and pour over enough boiled water to just cover them. Leave the tomatoes to soak for 15 minutes.

VARIATION
For a lower-fat version, you can leave out the Parmesan cheese and instead add diced red or yellow (bell) pepper with the chopped onion.

2 Lift the tomatoes out of the hot water and pat dry on kitchen paper. Reserve the soaking water. Use a sharp knife to cut the tomatoes into thin strips.

3 Heat the olive oil in a frying pan. Cook the onion for 5–6 minutes. Add the thyme and tomatoes and cook for a further 2–3 minutes.

4 Break the eggs into a bowl and beat lightly. Stir in 45ml/3 tbsp of the tomato soaking water and the Parmesan and season to taste.

5 Raise the heat and when the oil is sizzling, add the eggs. Mix quickly into the other ingredients. Lower the heat to medium and cook for 4–5 minutes, or until the base is golden.

6 Take a large plate, invert it over the pan and, holding it firmly, turn the pan and the frittata over on to it. Slide the frittata back into the pan, and cook for 3–4 minutes until golden brown on the second side.

7 Remove the pan from the heat. Cut the frittata into wedges and garnish with Parmesan shavings and thyme.

Egg frittata: Energy 170kcal/705kJ; Protein 5.7g; Carbohydrate 3g, of which sugars 2.6g; Fat 15.2g, of which saturates 4.1g; Cholesterol 13mg; Calcium 158mg; Fibre 0.6g; Sodium 167mg.

Smoked salmon with scrambled eggs

A classic combination, this breakfast also provides a great nutritious start to the day. With omega-3 fats from the salmon and the choline from the eggs, this is brain food at its best. Serve on wholemeal toast, to ensure that the energy will be released slowly throughout your morning.

Serves 4

15ml/1 tbsp rapeseed oil
2 onions, chopped
150-200g/5–7oz smoked salmon
   trimmings
6–8 eggs, lightly beaten
ground black pepper
45ml/3 tbsp chopped fresh chives,
   plus whole chives, to garnish
wholemeal (whole-wheat) toast or
   bagels, to serve

COOK'S TIP
If you don't have any smoked salmon, you can use fresh or canned salmon, which contains just as much omega-3 oil.

1 Heat the oil in a frying pan, then add the chopped onions and fry until they are softened and just beginning to brown.

2 Add the smoked salmon trimmings to the pan and mix well to combine with the onions.

3 Pour the eggs into the pan and stir until soft curds form. Stir off the heat until creamy. Season with pepper. Spoon on to serving plates and garnish with chopped and whole chives.

4 Serve the scrambled eggs immediately with hot buttered wholemeal toast or bagels.

Scrambled eggs: Energy 316kcal/1314kJ; Protein 22.8g; Carbohydrate 6.6g, of which sugars 0.8g; Fat 22.4g, of which saturates 8.2g; Cholesterol 249mg; Calcium 68mg; Fibre 0.3g; Sodium 231mg.

Grilled kippers with marmalade toast

The delicious smokiness of these cured herrings combines wonderfully with the tangy orange marmalade for a tasty and satisfying brunch dish. Herrings are one of the richest sources of omega-3 fats, which are excellent for keeping your heart healthy.

2 Using kitchen scissors or a knife, remove the heads and tails from the kippers.

3 Lay the fish, skin-side up, on the buttered foil. Put under the hot grill and cook for 1 minute. Turn the kippers over, brush the uppermost (fleshy) side with melted butter, put back under the grill and cook for 4–5 minutes.

Serves 2

melted butter, for greasing
2 kippers
2 slices of bread
soft butter, for spreading
orange marmalade, for spreading

1 Preheat the grill (broiler). Line the grill pan with foil – to help prevent fishy smells from lingering in the pan – and brush the foil with melted butter to stop the fish sticking.

4 Toast the bread and spread it first with butter and then with marmalade. Serve the sizzling hot kippers immediately with the marmalade on toast.

VARIATION
Omit the marmalade and cook the kippers sprinkled with a little cayenne pepper. Serve with a small knob (pat) of butter and plenty of lemon wedges for squeezing over.

Grilled kippers: Energy 518kcal/2155kJ; Protein 33.9g; Carbohydrate 17.6g, of which sugars 5.9g; Fat 35.1g, of which saturates 7.6g; Cholesterol 121mg; Calcium 126mg; Fibre 0.4g; Sodium 1640mg.

Smoked haddock with spinach and egg

This rich, high-protein breakfast dish is perhaps one for a weekend treat. Gently wilting the spinach will help retain its valuable nutrients, and serving with a glass of fruit juice will improve absorption of the iron from the spinach and eggs.

Serves 4

4 undyed smoked haddock fillets
milk, for poaching
45ml/3 tbsp low-fat Greek
   (US strained plain) yogurt
   or crème fraîche
250g/9oz fresh spinach, tough
   stalks removed
white wine vinegar
4 eggs
salt and ground black pepper

1 Put the haddock in a frying pan and pour in enough milk to come half-way up the fish. Poach the fillets over a low heat, shaking the pan gently, for 5 minutes.

2 Remove the fish from the pan and keep warm. Increase the heat and simmer the milk until it reduces by about half, stirring occasionally.

3 Stir the yogurt or crème fraîche into the milk. Heat through without letting the sauce boil. Season with pepper and remove from the heat.

4 Warm a frying pan over a gentle heat, add the spinach and allow to wilt for a few minutes. Season lightly with salt and pepper to taste, then set aside, keeping the leaves warm.

5 To poach the eggs, bring 4cm/1½in water to a simmer and add a few drops of vinegar. Gently crack two eggs into the water and cook for 3 minutes. Remove the first egg using a slotted spoon and rest the spoon on some kitchen paper to remove any water.

6 Repeat with the second egg, then cook the other two in the same way.

7 Place the spinach over the fillets and a poached egg on top. Pour over the cream sauce and serve immediately.

Smoked haddock: Energy 350kcal/1455kJ; Protein 27.5g; Carbohydrate 1.5g, of which sugars 1.4g; Fat 26.3g, of which saturates 14g; Cholesterol 277mg; Calcium 170mg; Fibre 1.3g; Sodium 969mg.

Oatmeal pancakes with bacon

A healthier alternative to a fry up, these savoury, oaty pancakes are perfect topped with a poached egg or grilled tomatoes. Use good-quality back bacon and cut off the rind to lower the fat content; the oats will help to reduce your cholesterol levels.

Makes 8

115g/4oz/1 cups wholemeal (whole-wheat) flour
25g/1oz/¼ cup fine pinhead oatmeal
pinch of salt
2 eggs
about 300ml/½ pint/1¼ cups buttermilk
butter or oil, for greasing
8 rashers (strips) back bacon

VARIATIONS
Try alternative fillings such as grilled mushrooms, smoked mackerel or salmon, or even jam.

---

1 Mix the flour, oatmeal and salt in a bowl or food processor, beat in the eggs and add enough buttermilk to make a creamy batter of the same consistency as ordinary pancakes.

2 Thoroughly heat a cast-iron frying pan or griddle over a medium heat. When very hot, grease lightly with butter or oil.

COOK'S TIP
When whole oats are chopped into pieces they are called pinhead or coarse oatmeal. They take longer to cook than rolled oats and have a chewier texture.

3 Pour in the batter, about a ladleful at a time. Tilt the pan around to spread the batter evenly and cook for about 2 minutes on the first side, or until set and the underside is browned.

4 Turn over and cook for about 1 minute until browned. Grill the bacon and tuck inside the cooked pancakes.

Oatmeal pancakes: Energy 202kcal/845kJ; Protein 11.9g; Carbohydrate 17.8g, of which sugars 2g; Fat 11.8g, of which saturates 4.8g; Cholesterol 87mg; Calcium 59mg; Fibre 1.5g; Sodium 654mg.

Kidney and mushroom toasts

Kidneys are an excellent, cheap source of many valuable nutrients including a highly absorbable form of iron. They are very quick and easy to cook and, served with tomatoes and mushrooms on wholemeal (whole-wheat) toast, make a tasty, filling breakfast.

Serves 4

4 large, flat field (portabello)
  mushrooms, stalks trimmed
50g/2oz/¼ cup butter
10ml/2 tsp wholegrain mustard
15ml/1 tbsp chopped fresh parsley
4 lamb's kidneys, skinned, halved
  and cored
4 thick slices of wholemeal (whole-
  wheat) bread, toasted
sprig of parsley, to garnish
tomato wedges, to serve

COOK'S TIP
Before cooking kidneys, remove the white core of membrane and tubes found in the centre.

1 Wash the mushrooms thoroughly and gently remove the stalks.

2 Blend the butter, wholegrain mustard and chopped fresh parsley together in a bowl.

3 Rinse the prepared lamb's kidneys well under cold running water, and pat dry with kitchen paper.

4 Melt the butter mixture in a large frying pan and fry the mushrooms and kidneys for about 3 minutes on each side.

5 When the kidneys are cooked to your liking (they taste best when left a little pink in the centre). Serve with the tomato, garnished with parsley, on the hot toast.

Kidney and mushroom toasts: Energy 593Kcal/2480kJ; Protein 39.2g; Carbohydrate 26.3g, of which sugars 2.7g; Fat 37.7g, of which saturates 21.6g; Cholesterol 647mg; Calcium 145mg; Fibre 4.3g; Sodium 773mg.

SOUPS, DIPS AND APPETIZERS

Warming, nutritious and sustaining, home-made soup is the
perfect health food. Light to eat, but with substantial food value,
it is ideal as a winter warmer. Soup can be cooked ahead, made
in big batches, chilled for several days or frozen for months – it is
practical, versatile and extremely good for you. This selection of
dips and appetizers is equally tempting and packed with highly
nutritious ingredients. Choose from a varied selection including
Artichoke and Cumin Dip, Marinated Tofu and Broccoli with
Shallots, Seaweed Sushi Rolls, and Garlic Prawns in Filo Tartlets.

Chilled avocado soup with cumin

This tasty cold soup combines creamy avocados with the distinctive flavours of onions, garlic, lemon and cumin. While avocado contains fat, it is the healthy monounsaturated type that can help to lower blood cholesterol levels. Aromatic cumin contains flavonoids that help to alleviate indigestion.

Serves 4

3 ripe avocados
a bunch of spring onions
   (scallions), white parts only,
   trimmed and roughly chopped
2 garlic cloves, chopped
juice of 1 lemon
1.5ml/¼ tsp ground cumin
1.5ml/¼ tsp paprika
450ml/¾ pint/scant 2 cups fresh
   vegetable stock
300ml/½ pint/1¼ cups iced water
ground black pepper
roughly chopped fresh flat leaf
   parsley, to garnish

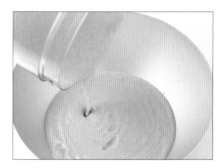

1 Starting half a day ahead, put the flesh of one avocado in a food processor or blender. Add the spring onions, garlic and lemon juice and purée until smooth. Add the second avocado and purée, then add the third, along with the spices and seasoning. Purée until smooth.

2 Gradually add the vegetable stock. Pour the soup into a metal bowl and chill for 2–3 hours.

3 To serve, stir in the iced water, then season to taste with plenty of black pepper. Garnish with chopped parsley and serve immediately.

Chilled avocado soup: Energy 220Kcal/907kJ; Protein 2.7g; Carbohydrate 2.9g, of which sugars 1.3g; Fat 21.8g, of which saturates 4.7g; Cholesterol 0mg; Calcium 22mg; Fibre 4.2g; Sodium 9mg.

Classic gazpacho

Raw tomatoes, cucumber and peppers form the basis of this classic chilled soup. Not cooking the vegetables retains all the vitamin C. Serving with a spoonful of chunky, fresh avocado salsa will add to the impressive fruit and vegetable count of this dish.

Serves 6

900g/2lb ripe tomatoes, peeled
  and seeded
1 cucumber, peeled and
  roughly chopped
2 red (bell) peppers, seeded and
  roughly chopped
2 garlic cloves, crushed
1 large onion, roughly chopped
30ml/2 tbsp white wine vinegar
120ml/4fl oz/½ cup olive oil
250g/9oz/4½ cups fresh white
  breadcrumbs
450ml/¾ pint/scant 2 cups
  iced water
salt and ground black pepper
12 ice cubes, to serve

For the garnish
30–45ml/2–3 tbsp olive oil
4 thick slices bread, crusts
  removed and cut into
  small cubes
2 tomatoes, peeled, seeded
  and finely diced
1 small green (bell) pepper,
  seeded and finely diced
1 small onion, very finely sliced
a small bunch of fresh flat leaf
  parsley, chopped

1 In a large bowl, mix the tomatoes, cucumber, peppers, garlic and onion. Stir in the vinegar, oil, breadcrumbs and water until well mixed.

3 To make the garnish, heat the oil in a frying pan and add the bread cubes. Cook over a medium heat for 5–6 minutes, stirring occasionally to brown evenly. Drain on kitchen paper and put into a small bowl.

4 Ladle the gazpacho into bowls and add two ice cubes to each, then serve immediately. Pass around the bowls of garnishing ingredients so that they can be added to suit individual taste.

2 Purée the mixture in a food processor or blender until almost smooth and pour into a large bowl. If the soup is too thick, add a little cold water. Stir in salt and pepper to taste and chill.

SUPERFOOD TIP
The powerful mix of fresh raw tomatoes, cucumbers, peppers, garlic, onion, and olive oil boosts circulation and the immune system and cleanses the body.

Classic gazpacho: Energy 244kcal/1009kJ; Protein 3g; Carbohydrate 12g, of which sugars 11g; Fat 21g, of which saturates 3g; Cholesterol 0mg; Calcium 34mg; Fibre 3.9g; Sodium 84mg.

Roasted garlic and butternut squash soup

Roasting the garlic mellows its strong flavour and enables you to eat more of this wonderful little bulb of goodness. Combined with the roasted butternut squash, a good source of vitamin A, it makes for a rich, filling soup without the need to add cream.

Serves 4

2 garlic bulbs, papery skin removed
75ml/5 tbsp olive oil
a few fresh thyme sprigs
1 large butternut squash, halved and seeded
2 onions, chopped
5ml/1 tsp ground coriander
1.2 litres/2 pints/5 cups vegetable or chicken stock
30–45ml/2–3 tbsp chopped fresh oregano or marjoram
salt and ground black pepper

For the salsa

4 large ripe tomatoes, halved and seeded
1 red (bell) pepper, halved and seeded
1 large fresh red chilli, halved and seeded
30–45ml/2–3 tbsp extra virgin olive oil
15ml/1 tbsp balsamic vinegar
pinch of caster (superfine) sugar

1 Preheat the oven to 220°C/425°F/Gas 7. Place the garlic bulbs on a piece of foil and pour over half the olive oil. Add the thyme sprigs, then fold the foil around the garlic bulbs.

2 Place the foil parcel and butternut squash on a baking sheet. Brush the squash with 15ml/1 tbsp of the rest of the olive oil. Add the tomatoes, red pepper and fresh chilli for the salsa.

3 Roast the vegetables for 25 minutes, then remove the tomatoes, pepper and chilli. Reduce the temperature to 190°C/375°F/Gas 5 and cook the squash and garlic for 20–25 minutes more, or until the squash is tender.

4 Heat the remaining oil in a large, heavy-based pan and cook the onions and ground coriander gently for about 10 minutes, or until they are softened.

5 Skin the pepper and chilli and process in a food processor or blender with the tomatoes and 30ml/2 tbsp olive oil. Stir in the vinegar and seasoning to taste, adding a pinch of caster sugar, if necessary. Add the remaining oil if you think the salsa needs it.

6 Squeeze the roasted garlic out of its papery skin into the onions and scoop the squash out of its skin, adding it to the pan. Add the stock, 5ml/1 tsp salt and plenty of black pepper. Bring to the boil and simmer for 10 minutes.

7 Stir in half the oregano or marjoram and cool the soup slightly, then process it in a blender or food processor. Alternatively, press the soup through a fine sieve (strainer).

8 Reheat the soup without allowing it to boil, then taste for seasoning before ladling it into warmed bowls. Top each with a spoonful of salsa and sprinkle over the remaining chopped oregano or marjoram. Serve immediately.

Butternut squash soup: Energy 238Kcal/986kJ; Protein 2.9g; Carbohydrate 11.9g, of which sugars 10.3g; Fat 20.2g of which saturates 3.1g; Cholesterol 0mg; Calcium 79mg; Fibre 4.1g; Sodium 11mg.

Red bean soup with avocado salsa

This aromatic, warming soup is perfect comfort food for a cold day. The cooling avocado and lime salsa make a nutritious vegetarian meal with plenty of slow-release carbohydrate. It is very high in both soluble and insoluble fibre, giving it heart-healthy credentials.

Serves 6

30ml/2 tbsp olive oil
2 onions, chopped
2 garlic cloves, chopped
10ml/2 tsp ground cumin
1.5ml/¼ tsp cayenne pepper
15ml/1 tbsp paprika
15ml/1 tbsp tomato purée (paste)
2.5ml/½ tsp dried oregano
400g/14oz can chopped tomatoes
2 x 400g/14oz cans red kidney
  beans, drained and rinsed
900ml/1½ pints/3¾ cups water
salt and ground black pepper
Tabasco sauce, to serve

For the guacamole salsa
2 avocados
1 small red onion, finely chopped
1 green chilli, seeded and finely
  chopped
15ml/1 tbsp chopped fresh
  coriander (cilantro)
juice of 1 lime

1 Heat the oil in a large, heavy-based pan and add the onions and garlic. Cook for about 4–5 minutes, until softened. Add the cumin, cayenne and paprika, and cook for 1 minute, stirring constantly.

2 Stir in the tomato purée and cook for a few seconds, then stir in the oregano. Add the chopped tomatoes, kidney beans and water.

COOK'S TIP
Make this soup in a big batch and freeze in small portions, ready to thaw in the microwave for an instant lunch or supper.

3 Bring the tomato and bean mixture to the boil and simmer for 15–20 minutes. Cool the soup slightly, then purée it in a food processor or blender until smooth. Return the mixture to the rinsed-out pan and add seasoning to taste.

4 To make the guacamole salsa, halve, stone (pit) and peel the avocados, then dice them finely. Place them in a small bowl and gently, but thoroughly, mix with the chopped red onion and chilli, and the fresh coriander and lime juice.

5 Reheat the soup and serve, topped with a little guacamole salsa and a dash of Tabasco sauce as desired.

VARIATION
Instead of salsa, the reheated soup can be topped with a poached egg and strips of quickly sautéed red pepper.

Red bean soup: Energy 254kcal/1064kJ; Protein 10.8g; Carbohydrate 29.2g, of which sugars 9.1g; Fat 11.2g, of which saturates 2.1g; Cholesterol 0mg; Calcium 111mg; Fibre 10.6g; Sodium 535mg.

Miso broth with tofu

This flavoursome broth is extremely nutritious, being high in protein and low in fat. Tofu and miso are both good sources of cholesterol-reducing soya proteins, and tofu also contains vegetarian omega 3; all of these properties are thought to be important for keeping your heart healthy.

3 Heat the mixture over a low heat until boiling, then lower the heat and simmer for about 10 minutes. Strain the broth, return it to the pan and reheat until simmering. Add the green portion of the sliced spring onions or leeks to the soup with the pak choi or Asian greens and tofu. Cook for 2 minutes.

4 In a small bowl, combine the miso with a little soup, then stir the mixture into the pan. Add soy sauce to taste.

5 Coarsely chop the coriander leaves and stir most of them into the soup with the white part of the spring onions or leeks.

6 Cook for 1 minute, then ladle the soup into warmed bowls. Sprinkle with the remaining chopped coriander and the shredded fresh red chilli, if using, and serve immediately.

COOK'S TIP
Some rice cakes make a good accompaniment for the soup, but for a more substantial snack, add noodles and simmer for the time suggested on the packet.

Serves 4

a bunch of spring onions
   (scallions) or 5 baby leeks
15g/½oz fresh coriander (cilantro)
3 thin slices fresh root ginger
2 star anise
1 small dried red chilli
1.2 litres/2 pints/5 cups dashi or
   vegetable stock
225g/8oz pak choi (bok choy) or
   other Asian greens, thickly sliced
200g/7oz firm tofu, cut into
   2.5cm/1in cubes
60ml/4 tbsp red miso
30–45ml/2–3 tbsp Japanese
   soy sauce
1 fresh red chilli, seeded and
   shredded (optional)

1 Cut the coarse green tops off the spring onions or baby leeks and slice the rest of the spring onions or leeks finely on the diagonal.

2 Place the spring onion or baby leek green tops in a large pan with the stalks from the coriander, ginger, star anise, dried chilli and the stock.

Miso broth with tofu: Energy 71kcal/297kJ; Protein 7.2g; Carbohydrate 4.2g, of which sugars 3.5g; Fat 2.9g, of which saturates 0.4g; Cholesterol 0mg; Calcium 372mg; Fibre 2.6g; Sodium 884mg.

Shiitake mushroom and red onion laksa

This hot-and-sour noodle soup is low in fat and calories, making it a good light lunch option. It is bursting with the flavour of the shiitake mushrooms, which are reputed to have cholesterol-reducing and anti-cancer properties. For a more hearty option use thick rice noodles instead of rice vermicelli.

Serves 6

150g/5oz/2½ cups dried shiitake
  mushrooms
1.2 litres/2 pints/5 cups boiling
  vegetable stock
30ml/2 tbsp tamarind paste
250ml/8fl oz/1 cup hot water
6 large dried red chillies, stems
  removed and seeded
2 lemon grass stalks, finely sliced
5ml/1 tsp ground turmeric
15ml/1 tbsp grated fresh galangal
1 onion, chopped
5ml/1 tsp dried shrimp paste
30ml/2 tbsp oil
10ml/2 tsp palm sugar
175g/6oz rice vermicelli
1 red onion, very finely sliced
1 small cucumber, seeded and cut
  into strips
a handful of fresh mint leaves,
  to garnish

1 Place the mushrooms in a bowl and pour in enough boiling stock to cover them, then leave to soak for about 30 minutes.

2 Put the tamarind paste in a bowl and pour in the hot water. Mash the paste with a fork to extract as much flavour as possible. Strain and reserve the liquid, discarding the pulp.

3 Soak the chillies in enough hot water to cover for 5 minutes, then drain, reserving the soaking liquid.

4 Process the lemon grass, turmeric, galangal, onion, soaked chillies and shrimp paste in a food processor or blender, adding a little soaking water from the chillies to form a paste.

5 Heat the oil in a large, heavy pan and cook the paste over a low heat for 4–5 minutes until fragrant.

6 Add the tamarind liquid and bring to the boil, then simmer for 5 minutes. Remove from the heat. Drain the mushrooms and reserve the stock.

7 Discard the stems of the mushrooms, then halve or quarter them, if large. Add the mushrooms to the pan together with their soaking liquid, the remaining stock and the palm sugar. Simmer for 25–30 minutes, or until the mushrooms are tender.

8 Put the rice vermicelli into a large bowl and cover with boiling water, then leave to soak for 4 minutes or according to the packet instructions.

9 Drain well, then divide among six bowls. Top with onion and cucumber, then ladle in the boiling shiitake soup. Add a small bunch of mint leaves to each bowl and serve immediately.

Shiitake mushroom laksa: Energy 146kcal/611kJ; Protein 4.4g; Carbohydrate 27.1g, of which sugars 3.7g; Fat 2.3g, of which saturates 0.3g; Cholesterol 4mg; Calcium 27mg; Fibre 1g; Sodium 54mg.

Chicken rice soup with lemon grass

This wholesome chicken rice soup is light and refreshing, with the fragrant aroma of lemon grass. The rice and shredded chicken are both easy to digest and this low-fat, low-calorie recipe makes a perfect pick-me-up if you have been under the weather.

Serves 4

1 small chicken or 2 meaty
  chicken legs
2 lemon grass stalks, trimmed, cut
  into 3 pieces, and lightly bruised
15ml/1 tbsp Thai fish sauce, such
  as nam pla
90g/3½oz/½ cup short grain
  rice, rinsed
1 small bunch coriander (cilantro)
  leaves, finely chopped, and
  1 green or red chilli, seeded and
  cut into thin strips, to garnish
1 lime, cut in wedges, to serve
sea salt
ground black pepper

For the stock
1 onion, quartered
2 cloves garlic, crushed
25g/1oz fresh root ginger, sliced
2 lemon grass stalks, cut in half
  lengthwise and bruised
2 dried red chillies
30ml/2 tbsp Thai dipping sauce

1 Put the chicken in a deep pan. Add all the stock ingredients and pour in 2 litres/3½ pints/7¾ cups water. Bring to the boil for a few minutes, then reduce the heat and simmer gently with the lid on for 2 hours.

2 Skim off any fat from the stock, strain and reserve. Remove the skin from the chicken and shred the meat. Set aside.

3 Pour the stock back into the deep pan and bring to the boil. Reduce the heat and stir in the lemon grass stalks and fish sauce. Stir in the rice and simmer, uncovered, for about 40 minutes.

4 Add the shredded chicken and season to taste. Ladle the piping hot soup into warmed individual bowls, garnish with chopped coriander and the thin strips of chilli, and serve with lime wedges to squeeze over.

Chicken rice soup: Energy 147Kcal/615kJ; Protein 12.8g; Carbohydrate 19.8g, of which sugars 1.4g; Fat 1.7g, of which saturates 0.4g; Cholesterol 53mg; Calcium 37mg; Fibre 0.8g; Sodium 320mg.

Guacamole

This simple, tasty dish is popular with many, including children who love to dip. Full of heart-healthy monounsaturated fats, the avocados provide a creamy base for the dip without the need to use cream or mayonnaise. Serve with a variety of vegetable crudités to enhance its superfood credentials.

Serves 6

2 large, ripe avocados
2 red chillies, seeded
1 garlic clove
1 shallot
30ml/2 tbsp extra virgin olive oil,
   plus extra to serve
juice of 1 lemon or lime
salt and ground black pepper
flat leaf parsley leaves, to garnish
vegetable crudités, such as
   cucumber, carrot, red pepper
   and celery, to serve

1 Cut the avocados in half and carefully remove the stones.

2 Scoop out the avocado flesh into a large mixing bowl, then using a fork or potato masher, mash the avocado flesh until smooth.

3 Finely chop the seeded chillies, garlic and shallot, then stir them into the mashed avocado with the olive oil and lemon or lime juice. Season to taste.

4 Spoon the mixture into a small serving bowl. Drizzle over a little extra olive oil and sprinkle with a few flat leaf parsley leaves. Serve the dip immediately.

COOK'S TIP
In order to store the guacamole before serving, place it in a container with a lid and refrigerate. This will slow down the browning of the avocado.

SUPERFOOD TIP
Although already bursting with superfoods, you can further enhance the nutritional content of the guacamole dip, by adding finely chopped vegetables such as tomatoes or green or red (bell) peppers just before serving. Not only will it boost the vitamin content of the dish, it will also add colour and a deliciously crunchy texture.

Guacamole: Energy 172kcal/709kJ; Protein 1g; Carbohydrate 2g, of which sugars 1g; Fat 18g, of which saturates 3g; Cholesterol 0mg; Calcium 9mg; Fibre 0.1g; Sodium 70mg.

Artichoke and cumin dip

This dip is so easy to make and is extremely tasty. Artichokes are an excellent source of fibre and also contain cynarin, which helps to keep the liver healthy. Served with olives, hummus and wedges of pitta bread, this makes a healthy Mediterranean lunch plate.

Serves 4

2 x 400g/14oz cans artichoke
   hearts, drained
2 garlic cloves, peeled
2.5ml/½ tsp ground cumin
olive oil
salt and ground black pepper

COOK'S TIP
To enjoy hot, spread the dip over a flat serving dish and sprinkle with grated cheese. Grill for 5 minutes or until warmed through.

1 Put the artichoke hearts in a food processor with the garlic and ground cumin, and a generous drizzle of olive oil. Process to a smooth purée and season with plenty of salt and ground black pepper to taste.

2 Spoon the purée into a serving bowl and drizzle an extra swirl of olive oil on the top. Serve the artichoke and cumin dip with raw vegetables and slices of warm pitta bread for dipping.

Artichoke and cumin dip: Energy 42Kcal/172kJ; Protein 0.6g; Carbohydrate 1.2g, of which sugars 0.9g; Fat 3.9g, of which saturates 0.5g: Cholesterol 0mg: Calcium 41mg: Fibre 1.2g: Sodium 60mg.

Chilli bean dip

This creamy and spicy bean dip is best served warm with triangles of grilled pitta bread or a bowl of crunchy tortilla chips. The beans are high in fibre and protein and the chillies contain phytochemicals, which are stimulants and can help boost circulation.

Serves 4

2 garlic cloves
1 onion
2 green chillies
30ml/2 tbsp vegetable oil
5–10ml/1–2 tsp hot chilli powder
400g/14oz can kidney beans
75g/3oz mature Cheddar
   cheese, grated
1 red chilli, seeded
salt and pepper

1 Finely chop the garlic and onion. Seed and chop the green chillies.

2 Heat the oil in a large pan. Add the garlic, onion, green chillies and chilli powder. Cook gently for 5 minutes, stirring regularly, until the onions are softened and transparent.

COOK'S TIP
Always handle chillies peppers with care as they can irritate the skin and eyes.

3 Drain the kidney beans, reserving the liquid. Blend all but 30ml/2 tbsp of the beans to a purée with a food processor or hand blender or, for a coarser texture, simply mash them.

4 Add the puréed beans to the pan with 30–45ml/2–3 tbsp of the reserved liquor. Heat gently, stirring to mix well.

5 Stir in the whole beans and the Cheddar cheese. Cook gently for 2–3 minutes, stirring until the cheese melts. Add salt and pepper to taste.

6 Cut the red chilli into tiny strips. Spoon the dip into four individual serving bowls and sprinkle the chilli strips over the top. Serve warm with toasted pitta bread or tortilla chips.

Chilli bean dip: Energy 240Kcal/1002kJ; Protein 12.3g; Carbohydrate 20.3g, of which sugars 5.4g; Fat 12.3g, of which saturates 4.8g: Cholesterol 18mg: Calcium 219mg: Fibre 6.6g: Sodium 527mg.

Hummus

There are hundreds of recipes for hummus, but the one constant is the chickpea. Containing high-quality protein and an impressive array of vitamins and minerals, this creamy dip is an excellent addition to a healthy diet. Serve with vegetable crudités and pitta bread for a light lunch or supper.

Serves 4–6

225g/8oz dried chickpeas, soaked
  in water for at least 6 hours,
  or 2 x 400g/14oz cans chickpeas,
  drained
45–60ml/3–4 tbsp olive oil
juice of 1–2 lemons
2 garlic cloves crushed
5ml/1 tsp cumin seeds
15–30ml/1–2 tbsp natural (plain)
  bio-yogurt
salt and ground black pepper
15ml/1 tbsp olive oil and paprika,
  to garnish

1 If using dried chickpeas, drain and place them in a pan with plenty of water. Bring to the boil, reduce the heat, cover and simmer for about 1½ hours, or until they are very soft. Drain.

2 Remove any loose skins by rubbing the chickpeas in a clean kitchen towel. Put the cooked chickpeas into a food processor or blender and process to a thick purée.

3 Add the olive oil, lemon juice, garlic and cumin seeds, and blend thoroughly. Add the yogurt to lighten the mixture, and season to taste. Adjust the hummus to your taste by adding a little more lemon or olive oil.

4 Transfer the hummus to a serving bowl and drizzle a little oil over the surface to keep it moist. Sprinkle a little paprika over the top of the hummus, and serve with warm bread or carrot and celery sticks.

Hummus: Energy 190kcal/798kJ; Protein 8.4g; Carbohydrate 19.3g, of which sugars 1.4g; Fat 9.4g, of which saturates 1.3g; Cholesterol 0mg; Calcium 70mg; Fibre 4.1g; Sodium 19mg.

Tofu falafels with hemp seed oil

Traditionally made from chickpeas, this version uses vegetarian omega-3-rich tofu and hemp seed oil as its base. These protein-rich, crunchy balls are great served with wholemeal pitta bread and a sweet chilli sauce. They are also a traditional accompaniment to hummus.

Serves 4–6

30ml/2 tbsp vegetable oil
2 large onions, finely chopped
3 garlic cloves, crushed
500g/1¼lb firm tofu, drained
200g/7oz/3¾ cups fresh
  breadcrumbs
15g/½oz bunch fresh parsley,
  finely chopped
15ml/1 tbsp hemp seed oil
45ml/3 tbsp soy sauce
50g/2oz/4 tbsp sesame seeds,
  toasted
5ml/1 tsp ground cumin
15ml/1 tbsp ground turmeric
60ml/4 tbsp tahini (see Cook's Tips)
juice of 1 lemon
1.5ml/¼ tsp cayenne pepper

VARIATION
For a quick alternative dip, mix 30ml/2 tbsp of crème fraîche with 15ml/1tbsp chopped mint.

COOK'S TIPS
• Tahini, a paste made from sesame seeds, can be bought from most supermarkets or health food shops.
• If you like, process the tofu in a blender or food processor to a smooth paste before mixing with the other ingredients.

1 Heat the vegetable oil in a large frying pan and sauté the onion and garlic over a medium heat for 2–3 minutes, until softened. Set aside to cool slightly.

2 Preheat the oven to 180°C/350°F/ Gas 4. In a large bowl, mix together the remaining ingredients until they are well blended, then stir in the onion mixture.

3 Form the mixture into 2.5cm/ 1in diameter balls and place them on an oiled baking sheet. Bake in the oven for 30 minutes, or until the balls are crusty on the outside but still moist on the inside.

4 Spear each of the hot falafels with a cocktail stick (toothpick), and serve immediately with a hummus dip and slices of warm pitta bread.

Falafels with hemp seed oil: Energy 341kcal/1422kJ; Protein 14g; Carbohydrate 22g, of which sugars 5g; Fat 23g, of which saturates 3g; Cholesterol 0mg; Calcium 611mg; Fibre 2.5g; Sodium 718mg.

Sprout salad with cashew cream dressing

This interesting salad has contrasting colours, textures and flavours and you can experiment with your own favourite sprout mix. The sprouts are very high in B-vitamins and vitamin C and the cashews and seeds are full of essential fatty acids, making this a highly nutritious salad.

2 Process the nuts with their soaking water in a food processor until you have a smooth sauce. Add more water if necessary.

3 Place the chopped pepper, sprouts, cucumber and lemon juice in a bowl and toss together. Serve with the cashew cream and sprinkle with the herbs and seeds.

COOK'S TIPS
• The cashew cream makes a smooth dressing for many different salads or can be used as a sauce. Cashews are rich in monounsaturated fatty acids, as found in the Mediterranean diet, and are favoured for their heart-protecting and anti-cancer properties.
• There are all kinds of sprouts, and beansprouts are one of the most readily commercially available. Rinse thoroughly in cold water before using in salads, juices and other recipes. Choose fresh, crisp sprouts with the seed or bean still attached. Avoid any that are slimy or appear musty. Sprouts are best eaten on the day they are bought, but, if fresh, they will keep for 2–3 days wrapped in a plastic bag in the refrigerator.

Serves 2

130g/4½oz cashew nuts
1 red (bell) pepper, seeded
   and finely chopped
90g/3½oz mung or aduki
   beansprouts or chickpea sprouts
½ small cucumber, chopped
juice of ½ lemon
small bunch fresh parsley,
   coriander (cilantro) or basil,
   finely chopped
5ml/1 tsp sesame, sunflower or
   pumpkin seeds

1 Soak the cashew nuts in 90ml/3½fl oz/6 tbsp of water for a few hours, preferably overnight, until they are plump.

Sprout salad with cashew cream: Energy 352Kcal/1459kJ; Protein 12g; Carbohydrate 18g; of which sugars 10g; Fat 26g; of which saturates 5g; Cholesterol 0mg; Calcium 78mg; Fibre 4.7g; Sodium 19mg.

Marinated tofu and broccoli with shallots

Gently steaming the tender young stems of broccoli retains their excellent nutritional content and, combined with marinated tofu, they make a very tasty and nourishing lunch. Sprinkling with shallots and sesame seeds further boosts the superfood content of this recipe.

Serves 4

500g/1¼lb block of firm
  tofu, drained
45ml/3 tbsp Indonesian soy sauce
30ml/2 tbsp sweet chilli sauce
45ml/3 tbsp soy sauce
5ml/1 tsp sesame oil
5ml/1 tsp finely grated fresh
  root ginger
400g/14oz tenderstem broccoli,
  halved lengthways
45ml/3 tbsp roughly chopped
  coriander (cilantro)
30ml/2 tbsp toasted sesame seeds
30ml/2 tbsp crispy fried shallots
steamed white rice or noodles,
  to serve

VARIATION
You could make this dish into a more substantial and satisfying meal by serving the tofu and broccoli with shallots and brown rice or buckwheat noodles.

1 Cut the tofu into four equal triangles. Place the tofu chunks in a heatproof dish.

2 In a small bowl, combine the soy sauce, chilli sauce, soy sauce, sesame oil and grated ginger. Pour over the tofu. Leave the tofu triangles to marinate for at least 30 minutes, turning them over occasionally.

3 Place the broccoli on a heatproof plate and place on a trivet or steamer rack in the wok. Cover and steam for 4–5 minutes, until just tender. Remove and keep warm.

4 Divide the broccoli among four warmed serving plates and top each one with a piece of tofu.

5 Spoon the remaining juices over the tofu and broccoli, then sprinkle over the coriander, sesame seeds and crispy shallots. Serve immediately with steamed white rice or noodles.

SUPERFOOD TIP
Firm tofu is good source of vegetarian omega-3 fats.

Marinated tofu: Energy 202Kcal/840kJ; Protein 16.5g; Carbohydrate 6.9g, of which sugars 5.6g; Fat 12.1g, of which saturates 1.7g; Cholesterol 0mg; Calcium 750mg; Fibre 3.5g; Sodium 938mg.

Red onion tart

Red onions have very high levels of flavonol antioxidants and are wonderfully mild and sweet when cooked slowly. The concentrated, caramelized onions make a juicy, sweet filling in this crumbly, buttery pastry case, and the fontina cheese is rich and creamy in contrast.

Serves 5–6

60ml/4 tbsp olive oil
1kg/2¼lb red onions, thinly sliced
2–3 garlic cloves, thinly sliced
5ml/1 tsp chopped fresh thyme,
  plus a few whole sprigs
5ml/1 tsp dark brown sugar
10ml/2 tsp sherry vinegar
225g/8oz fontina cheese,
  thinly sliced
salt and ground black pepper

For the pastry
115g/4oz/1 cup plain (all-purpose)
  flour
75g/3oz/¾ cup fine yellow
  cornmeal
5ml/1 tsp dark brown sugar
5ml/1 tsp chopped fresh thyme
90g/3½oz/7 tbsp butter
1 egg yolk
45ml/3 tbsp iced water

1 To make the pastry, sift the flour and cornmeal into a bowl with 5ml/ 1 tsp salt. Add plenty of black pepper and stir in the sugar and thyme. Rub in the butter until the mixture looks like breadcrumbs.

2 Beat the egg yolk with 30ml/ 2 tbsp iced water and use to bind the pastry, adding another 15ml/1 tbsp iced water, if necessary. Gather the dough into a ball with your fingertips, wrap and chill it for 30–40 minutes.

3 Heat 45ml/3 tbsp of the oil in a large, deep frying pan and add the onions. Cover and cook slowly, stirring occasionally, for 20–30 minutes. They should collapse but not brown.

4 Add the garlic and chopped thyme, then cook, stirring occasionally, for another 10 minutes. Increase the heat slightly, then add the sugar and sherry vinegar. Cook, uncovered, for another 5–6 minutes, until the onions start to caramelize slightly. Season to taste with salt and pepper. Cool.

5 Preheat the oven to 190°C/375°F/ Gas 5. Roll out the pastry thinly and use to line a 25cm/10in loose-based metal flan tin (quiche pan).

6 Prick the pastry all over with a fork and support the sides with foil. Bake for 12–15 minutes, or until it becomes lightly coloured.

7 Remove the foil and spread the caramelized onions evenly over the base of the pastry case (pie shell). Add the fontina and thyme and season with pepper.

8 Drizzle over the remaining oil, then bake for 15–20 minutes, until the filling is piping hot and the cheese is beginning to bubble. Garnish the tart with thyme and serve immediately. Serve with a tomato and basil salad.

Red onion tart: Energy 621kcal/2581kJ; Protein 18.1g; Carbohydrate 45.6g, of which sugars 12.5g; Fat 40.6g, of which saturates 20.7g; Cholesterol 122mg; Calcium 424mg; Fibre 3.8g; Sodium 443mg.

Roast peppers and tomatoes with sweet cicely

The aniseed flavours of sweet cicely and fennel combine beautifully with the succulent flavours of the roasted vegetables and the piquancy of capers. Rich in lycopene from red peppers and tomatoes, this dish is packed full of free-radical-neutralizing antioxidants.

Serves 4

4 red or yellow (bell) peppers,
    halved and seeded
8 small or 4 medium tomatoes
15ml/1 tbsp semi-ripe sweet
    cicely seeds
15ml/1 tbsp fennel seeds
15ml/1 tbsp capers, rinsed
4 sweet cicely flowers, newly
    opened, stems removed
60ml/4 tbsp olive oil
a few small sweet cicely leaves
    and 8 sweet cicely flowers,
        to garnish

1 Preheat the oven to 180°C/350°F/ Gas 4. Place the red pepper halves, skin side down, in a large ovenproof dish and set aside.

2 To skin the tomatoes, cut a cross at the base, then put in a bowl and pour over boiling water. Leave them to stand for 1 minute. Cut in half if they are of medium size, or leave whole if small. Place a whole small or half a medium tomato in each half of a pepper cavity.

VARIATION
If sweet cicely is not available, this dish can be made with a range of different herbs, such as chervil or lovage, although they will all impart a distinctive flavour.

3 Cover with a scattering of sweet cicely seeds, fennel seeds and capers and about half the sweet cicely flowers. Drizzle the olive oil all over. Bake in for 1 hour. Serve hot, garnished with fresh sweet cicely leaves and flowers.

Roast peppers: Energy 172Kcal/714kJ; Protein 2.5g; Carbohydrate 14.3g, of which sugars 13.8g; Fat 12g, of which saturates 1.9g; Cholesterol 0mg; Calcium 21mg; Fibre 3.8g; Sodium 16mg.

Herb and aduki bean-stuffed mushrooms

Portabello mushrooms have a rich flavour and a meaty texture that go well with this fragrant bean and herb stuffing. High in fibre and low in fat, beans add satisfying substance to this stuffing, and the garlicky pine nut accompaniment has a smooth, creamy consistency similar to that of hummus.

Serves 4–6

200g/7oz/1 cup dried or
    400g/14oz/2 cups drained,
    canned aduki beans
45ml/3 tbsp olive oil, plus extra
    for brushing
1 onion, finely chopped
2 garlic cloves, crushed
30ml/2 tbsp fresh chopped or
    5ml/1 tsp dried thyme
8 large field (portabello)
    mushrooms, stalks finely
    chopped
50g/2oz/1 cup fresh wholemeal
    (whole-wheat) breadcrumbs
juice of 1 lemon
185g/6½oz/¾ cup goat's cheese,
    crumbled
salt and freshly ground black
    pepper

For the pine nut tarator
50g/2oz/½ cup pine nuts toasted
50g/2oz/1 cup cubed white bread
2 garlic cloves, chopped
200ml/7fl oz/1 cup semi-skimmed
    (low-fat) milk
45ml/3 tbsp olive oil
15ml/1 tbsp chopped fresh parsley,
    to garnish (optional)

1 If using dried beans, soak them overnight, then drain and rinse well. Place in a pan, add enough water to cover and bring to the boil. Boil rapidly for 10 minutes, then reduce the heat, cook for 30 minutes, until tender, then drain. If using canned beans, rinse, drain well, then set aside.

2 Preheat the oven to 200°C/400°F/ Gas 6. Heat the oil in a frying pan, add the onion and garlic and sauté for 5 minutes, until softened. Add the thyme and the mushroom stalks and cook for a further 3 minutes, stirring occasionally, until tender.

3 Stir in the beans, breadcrumbs and lemon juice, season well, then cook for 2 minutes, until heated through. Mash two-thirds of the beans with a fork or potato masher, leaving the remaining beans whole.

4 Brush a baking dish and the base and sides of the mushrooms with oil, then top each one with a spoonful of the bean mixture. Put the mushrooms in the dish, cover with foil and bake for 20 minutes. Remove the foil. Top each mushroom with goat's cheese and bake for a further 15 minutes.

5 To make the pine nut tarator, blend all the ingredients until smooth and creamy. Add more milk if the mixture appears too thick. Sprinkle with parsley and serve with the mushrooms.

SUPERFOOD TIP
All beans are high in protein and fibre, and low in fat. They also contain some B vitamins and iron.

Stuffed mushrooms: Energy 406Kcal/1694kJ; Protein 17.5g; Carbohydrate 25.9g, of which sugars 5.9g; Fat 26.6g, of which saturates 8g; Cholesterol 31mg; Calcium 159mg; Fibre 6.1g; Sodium 573mg.

Leek terrine with red peppers

This attractive pressed leek and pepper terrine is a tasty summer salad dish. Both leeks and peppers are rich in antioxidants and fibre, both of which may contribute to a reduced cancer risk. The olive oil-rich dressing also contains heart-healthy monosaturated fats.

Serves 6–8

1.8kg/4lb slender leeks
4 large red (bell) peppers, halved
  and seeded
15ml/1 tbsp extra virgin olive oil
10ml/2 tsp balsamic vinegar
5ml/1 tsp ground roasted
  cumin seeds
salt and ground black pepper

For the dressing
120ml/4fl oz/½ cup extra virgin
  olive oil
1 garlic clove, bruised and peeled
5ml/1 tsp Dijon mustard
5ml/1 tsp soy sauce
15ml/1 tbsp balsamic vinegar
pinch of caster (superfine) sugar
2.5–5ml/½–1 tsp ground roasted
  cumin seeds
15–30ml/1–2 tbsp chopped mixed
  fresh basil and flat leaf parsley

1 Line a 23cm/9in-long terrine or loaf tin (pan) with clear film, leaving the ends overhanging the tin. Cut each of the leeks to the same length as the tin.

2 Cook the leeks in boiling salted water for 5–7 minutes, until just tender. Drain thoroughly and allow to cool, then squeeze out as much water as possible from the leeks and leave them to drain on a clean dish towel.

3 Grill the red peppers, skin-side uppermost, until the skin blisters and blackens. Place in a bowl, cover and leave for 10 minutes. Peel the peppers and cut the flesh into long strips, then place them in a bowl and add the oil, balsamic vinegar and ground roasted cumin. Season to taste with salt and pepper and toss well.

4 Layer the leeks and strips of red pepper in the lined tin, alternating the layers so that the white of the leeks in one row is covered by the green of the next row. Season the leeks with a little salt and pepper.

5 Cover the terrine with the overhanging clear film. Top with a plate and weigh it down with heavy food cans or scale weights. Chill for several hours or overnight.

6 To make the dressing, place the oil, garlic, mustard, soy sauce and vinegar in a jug and mix thoroughly. Season and add the caster sugar. Add the ground cumin seeds to taste and leave to stand for several hours. Discard the garlic and add the fresh herbs to the dressing.

7 Unmould the terrine and cut it into thick slices. Put 1–2 slices on each plate, drizzle with dressing and serve.

Leek terrine with red peppers: Energy 171Kcal/710kJ; Protein 4.6g; Carbohydrate 12.4g, of which sugars 10.5g; Fat 11.7g, of which saturates 1.8g; Cholesterol 0mg; Calcium 66mg; Fibre 6.4g; Sodium 161mg.

Smoked mackerel pâté

One of the most convenient sources of heart-healthy omega-3 fats, smoked mackerel is cheap and widely available, and so it makes a great way to boost your oily fish intake. Making this pâté couldn't be quicker or easier and is a sure-fire winner with children and adults alike.

Serves 4–6

225g/8oz/1 cup crème fraîche or
    Greek (US strained plain) yogurt
finely grated rind of ½ lemon
few sprigs of parsley
225g/8oz smoked mackerel fillets
5–10ml/1–2 tsp horseradish sauce
1 tbsp lemon juice, or to taste
ground black pepper
crusty bread, hot toast or crisp
    plain crackers, to serve
lemon wedges, to serve

COOK'S TIP
To turn this recipe into a dip, just add a little more crème fraîche until it is of the desired consistency.

---

1 Place the crème fraîche or Greek yogurt and grated lemon rind into a blender or food processor. Add a few sprigs of parsley.

2 Flake the mackerel, discarding the skin and any bones. Add the flaked fish to the blender. Blend on a medium speed until the mixture is almost smooth.

3 Add the horseradish sauce and lemon juice and blend briefly. Season with ground black pepper. Spoon the mackerel pâté into individual dishes. Cover and refrigerate.

4 Garnish with parsley and serve with warm crusty bread, hot toast or crisp plain crackers, and lemon wedges for squeezing over.

Smoked mackerel pâté: Energy 344kcal/1421kJ; Protein 10.7g; Carbohydrate 0.5g, of which sugars 0.4g; Fat 33.3g, of which saturates 14.3g; Cholesterol 88mg; Calcium 57mg; Fibre 0.1g; Sodium 518mg.

Tuna and wasabi

Unlike its canned counterpart, fresh tuna is an excellent source of omega-3 fat that is proven to keep your heart healthy as well as to improve brain function. This marinated raw dish is a classic Japanese sashimi with a tremendous warming kick from the wasabi.

Serves 4

400g/14oz very fresh tuna, skinned
1 carton mustard and cress (optional)
20ml/4 tsp wasabi paste from a tube, or the same amount of wasabi powder mixed with 10ml/2 tsp water
60ml/4 tbsp Japanese soy sauce
8 spring onions (scallions), green part only, finely chopped
4 shiso leaves, cut into thin slivers lengthways

1 Cut the tuna into 2cm/¾in cubes. If you are using mustard and cress, tie it into pretty bunches or arrange as a bed in four small serving bowls or on plates.

2 Just 5–10 minutes before serving, blend the wasabi paste with the soy sauce in a bowl, then add the tuna and spring onions. Mix and leave to marinate for 5 minutes. Divide among the bowls and add a few slivers of shiso leaves on top. Serve immediately.

Tuna and wasabi: Energy 153Kcal/643kJ; Protein 24.5g; Carbohydrate 2.3g, of which sugars 2.1g; Fat 5.1g, of which saturates 1.3g; Cholesterol 29mg; Calcium 28mg; Fibre 0.4g; Sodium 806mg.

Seaweed sushi rolls

Nori is a type of sea vegetable that has been processed into sheets specifically for sushi making. It is packed full of essential minerals such as iodine, which is important in thyroid function. Add to the superfood count by filling the rolls with strips of salmon, tuna, avocado or pepper.

3 Place a sheet of nori, shiny-side down, on a bamboo mat. Divide the rice into 12 portions. Spread one portion over the nori, leaving a 1cm/½in clear space at the top and bottom.

4 Spread a little wasabi paste in a horizontal line along the middle of the rice and place one or two sticks of tuna on this.

Makes 12 rolls or 72 slices

400g/14oz/2 cups sushi rice, soaked for 20 minutes in water to cover
55ml/3½ tbsp rice vinegar
15ml/1 tbsp sugar
2.5ml/½ tsp salt
6 sheets nori seaweed
200g/7oz tuna, in one piece
200g/7oz salmon, in one piece
wasabi paste
½ cucumber, quartered lengthways and seeded
pickled ginger, to garnish (optional)
Japanese soy sauce, to serve

1 Drain the rice, then put in a pan with 525ml/18fl oz/2¼ cups water. Bring to the boil, then lower the heat, cover and simmer for 20 minutes, or until all the liquid has been absorbed. Meanwhile, heat the vinegar, sugar and salt, stir well and cool. Add to the hot rice, then remove the pan from the heat and allow to stand (covered) for 20 minutes.

2 Cut the nori sheets in half lengthways. Cut each of the tuna and salmon into four long sticks, about the same length as the long side of the nori, and about 1cm/½in square if viewed from the end.

5 Holding the mat and the edge of the yaki-nori nearest to you, roll up the seaweed and rice into a cylinder with the tuna in the middle. Use the mat as a guide – do not roll it into the food. Roll the rice tightly so that it sticks together and encloses the tuna.

6 Carefully roll the sushi off the mat. Make 11 more rolls in the same way, four for each filling ingredient, but do not use wasabi with the cucumber. Use a wet knife to cut each roll into six slices and stand them on a platter. Garnish with pickled ginger, if you wish, and serve with soy sauce.

Seaweed sushi rolls: Energy 31kcal/128kJ; Protein 1.7g; Carbohydrate 4.8g, of which sugars 0.3g; Fat 0.5g, of which saturates 0.1g; Cholesterol 2mg; Calcium 4mg; Fibre 0.1g; Sodium 3mg.

Garlic prawns in filo tartlets

These light, tasty tartlets are made with crisp golden layers of filo pastry and filled with spicy garlic and chilli prawns. Prawns are high in protein and low in fat, and when served with salad or new potatoes, make a well-balanced healthy meal.

Serves 4

For the tartlets
50g/2oz/4 tbsp butter, melted
2–3 large sheets filo pastry

For the filling
115g/4oz/½ cup butter
2–3 garlic cloves, crushed
1 red chilli, seeded and chopped
350g/12oz/3 cups cooked peeled
    prawns (shrimps)
30ml/2 tbsp chopped fresh parsley
    or chopped fresh chives
salt and freshly ground
    black pepper

1 Preheat the oven to 200°C/ 400°F/Gas 6. Brush four individual 7.5cm/3in flan tins (pans) with the melted butter.

2 Cut the filo pastry into twelve 10cm/4in squares and brush with the melted butter.

3 Place three squares of pastry inside each tin, overlapping them at slight angles and carefully frilling the edges and points, while at the same time forming a good hollow in the centre of each tartlet. Brush with a little more butter.

4 Bake in the oven for 10–15 minutes, until crisp and golden. Leave to cool slightly, then remove the pastry cases from the tins.

5 Meanwhile, make the filling. Melt the butter in a frying pan, then add the garlic, chilli and prawns and fry quickly for 1–2 minutes to warm through. Stir in the parsley or chives and season with salt and plenty of pepper. Spoon the prawn filling into the tartlets and serve at once.

COOK'S TIP
If you prefer your spicy food with a little more heat, then simply add another fresh chilli, or choose a hotter variety.

Garlic prawn tartlets: Energy 440kcal/1825kJ; Protein 17.6g; Carbohydrate 15g, of which sugars 0.7g; Fat 34.8g, of which saturates 21.6g; Cholesterol 259mg; Calcium 118mg; Fibre 1g; Sodium 419mg.

SALADS, SIDES AND DRESSINGS

Delicious salads, sides, salsas and dressings can be made from an endless variety of superfood ingredients, including vitamin-packed fruit and vegetables and protein-rich eggs, meat and oily fish. This chapter introduces a selection of vibrant recipes to enjoy either on their own or to complement a main dish. Choose from an enticing selection of dishes including Green Soya Bean and Rocket Salad, Watermelon and Feta Salad, Chilli Rice with Turmeric and Coriander, and Marinated Salmon with Avocado.

Tricolore salad

A classic Italian salad, the key to making this perfectly is in using the best ingredients possible. Buffalo mozzarella has the best flavour and ripe plum tomatoes are ideal. Use a ripe but not too soft avocado and your best extra virgin olive oil; both will contribute heart-healthy monounsaturated oils.

Serves 2–3

150g/5oz mozzarella, thinly sliced
4 large plum tomatoes, sliced
1 large firm and ripe avocado
about 12 basil leaves or a
    small handful of flat leaf
    parsley leaves
45–60ml/3–4 tbsp extra virgin
    olive oil
ground black pepper
ciabatta and sea salt flakes,
    to serve

1 Arrange the sliced mozzarella cheese and tomatoes randomly on two salad plates. Crush over a few good pinches of sea salt flakes. This will help to draw out some of the juices from the plum tomatoes. Set aside in a cool place and leave to marinate for about 30 minutes.

2 Just before serving, cut the avocado in half using a sharp knife and twist the halves to separate. Lift out the stone (pit) and remove the peel.

3 Carefully slice the avocado flesh crossways into half moons, or cut it into large chunks if that is easier.

4 Place the avocado on the salad, then sprinkle with the basil or parsley. Drizzle over the olive oil, add a little more salt if needed and some ground black pepper.

5 Serve immediately, with chunks of crusty Italian ciabatta for mopping up the dressing.

Tricolore salad: Energy 526kcal/2180kJ; Protein 17.5g; Carbohydrate 8.3g, of which sugars 7.2g; Fat 47.1g, of which saturates 16g; Cholesterol 44mg; Calcium 344mg; Fibre 5.8g; Sodium 327mg.

Moroccan carrot salad

Grating and slicing carrot for use in salads is a very good way of ensuring that the antioxidant carotenes are released from the cell walls where they are bound up. Choose slender carrots and slice thinly, so they only need cooking for a few minutes, which preserves optimum nutrition levels.

Serves 4–6

3–4 carrots, thinly sliced
pinch of sugar
3–4 garlic cloves, chopped
1.5ml/¼ tsp ground cumin, or to taste
juice of ½ lemon
30–45ml/2–3 tbsp extra virgin olive oil
15–30ml/1–2 tbsp red wine vinegar or fruit vinegar, such as raspberry
30ml/2 tbsp chopped fresh coriander (cilantro) leaves, or a mixture of coriander and parsley
salt and ground black pepper

1 Cook the sliced carrots by either steaming or boiling in a little water until they are just tender but not too soft. Drain the carrots and leave for a few moments to dry off, then place them in a bowl.

2 In a measuring jug (cup) mix together the sugar, garlic, cumin, lemon juice, olive oil and vinegar then pour over the carrots and toss together. Add the chopped fresh herbs and season to taste. Serve warm or chilled.

Moroccan carrot salad: Energy 53Kcal/220kJ; Protein 0.6g; Carbohydrate 4.2g, of which sugars 3.9g; Fat 3.9g, of which saturates 0.6g; Cholesterol 0mg; Calcium 29mg; Fibre 1.6g; Sodium 15mg.

Blue cheese, fig and walnut salad

A classic combination of nuts and cheese, this is a delicious fresh-tasting first course that can also be served without the figs as a cheese course. High-fibre figs are loaded with minerals. Walnuts are an excellent source of vegetarian omega 3 and antioxidants, both of which are cardioprotective.

Serves 4

Mixed salad leaves
4 fresh figs
115g/4oz Roquefort or other
    soft blue cheese, cut into
    small chunks
75g/3oz/¾ cup walnut halves

For the dressing
45ml/3 tbsp walnut oil
juice of 1 lemon
salt and ground black pepper

1 Mix all the dressing ingredients together in a bowl. Whisk briskly until thick and emulsified.

2 Wash and dry the salad leaves, then tear them gently into bitesize pieces. Place in a mixing bowl and toss with the dressing.

3 Transfer to a large serving dish or divide among four individual plates, ensuring a good balance of colour and texture on each plate.

COOK'S TIP
If you are trying to reduce your intake of saturated fats, use half the recommended amount of blue cheese. Blue cheese has a strong flavour, so a little will go a long way.

4 Cut the figs into quarters and add to the salad leaves.

5 Sprinkle the cheese over, crumbling it slightly. Then sprinkle over the walnuts, breaking them up roughly in your fingers as you go.

VARIATION
The figs may be replaced with ripe nectarines or peaches if you prefer. Wash and cut in half, discard the stone (pit), then cut each half into three or four slices. If the skin is tough, you may need to remove it.

Blue cheese and walnut salad: Energy 415kcal/1726kJ; Protein 10.6g; Carbohydrate 26.6g, of which sugars 26.4g; Fat 30.3g, of which saturates 7.3g; Cholesterol 22mg; Calcium 286mg; Fibre 4.5g; Sodium 383mg.

Watercress and pear salad with cheese dressing

A refreshing light salad, this dish combines lovely peppery watercress, soft juicy pears and a tart but creamy dressing. Watercress has high antioxidant levels and sulphur-containing phytonutrients, which together make a powerful combination.

Serves 4

25g/1oz soft blue cheese (Danish
  Blue, Roquefort or Gorganzola)
30ml/2 tbsp walnut oil
15ml/1 tbsp lemon juice
2 bunches of watercress,
  thoroughly washed
  and trimmed
2 ripe pears (see Cook's Tips)
salt and ground black pepper

1 Crumble and then mash the blue cheese into the walnut oil.

2 Whisk in the lemon juice to create a thickish mixture. If you need to thicken it further, add a little more cheese. Season to taste with salt and black pepper. Arrange a pile of watercress on the side of four plates.

SUPERFOOD TIP
Pears are a good source of both soluble and insoluble fibre, as well as vitamin C and potassium.

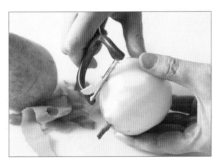

3 Just before serving, peel and slice the two pears, then place the pear slices to the side of the watercress, allowing half a pear per person. You can also put the pear slices on top of the watercress, if you prefer. Drizzle the dressing over the salad.

COOK'S TIPS
• Choose Comice or similar pears that are soft and juicy for this salad.
• If you want to get things ready in advance, peel and slice the pears, then rub them with some lemon juice in order to stop them from discolouring so quickly.
• If you find the flavour of the watercress is too strong on its own, you can try mixing it with baby spinach leaves or rocket (arugula) leaves to vary the taste.

Watercress and pear salad: Energy 106kcal/442kJ; Protein 2.3g; Carbohydrate 7.6g, of which sugars 7.6g; Fat 7.6g, of which saturates 1.8g; Cholesterol 5mg; Calcium 81mg; Fibre 2g; Sodium 91mg.

Green soya bean and rocket salad

This quick and simple salad is a refreshing change from mere leaves, as these young beans give a lovely texture. As well as being an excellent source of protein for vegetarians and vegans, green soya beans also contain cholesterol-reducing isoflavones.

Serves 4

250g/9oz green soya beans
70g/2¾oz rocket (arugula) leaves
10ml/2 tsp fresh basil leaves
2 tsp fresh coriander (cilantro)
  leaves
1 tbsp olive oil
1 tsp lemon juice
1 tsp balsamic vinegar
fresh ground black pepper

COOK'S TIP
Green soya beans are also known as edamame beans. You can buy them frozen for convenience.

1 Cook the soya beans in boiling water for 5 minutes. Drain, then set aside to cool. Chop the fresh rocket, basil and coriander leaves.

2 To make the dressing, mix together the olive oil, lemon juice and vinegar. Season with ground black pepper.

3. When the beans are cool, pour over the dressing and stir to mix both well together.

4 Toss the dressed beans together with the rocket and chopped herbs. Serve the salad immediately.

Green soya bean and rocket salad: Energy 125Kcal/520kJ; Protein 9g; Carbohydrate 4g, of which sugars 2g; Fat 8g, of which saturates 1g; Cholesterol 0mg; Calcium 59mg; Fibre 4g; Sodium 1mg.

Grated carrot, apple and alfalfa sprout salad

This refreshingly sweet and fragrant salad looks colourful and tastes good with its fat-free lemon juice and honey dressing. Grating improves the availability of all the phytonutrients, and the nutrient-rich alfalfa sprouts add a delightful nutty flavour.

Serves 1

90g/3½oz carrots, peeled and
  coarsely grated
2 desert apples, coarsely grated
2.5cm/1in piece fresh root ginger,
  peeled and finely grated
juice of ½ lemon or 15ml/
  1 tbsp cider apple vinegar
5ml/1 tsp clear honey
small handful alfalfa or
  other beansprouts of
  your choice
5ml/1 tsp sesame seeds, to
  serve (optional)

1 Place the grated carrots, apples and ginger in a large bowl. Add the lemon juice or cider apple vinegar and the clear honey, and mix all of the ingredients well together.

2 Transfer the mixed ingredients to a small bowl and press down firmly.

3 Carefully invert the bowl on to a plate to make a neat 'castle'. Top this with the alfalfa, and sprinkle liberally with sesame seeds to serve.

COOK'S TIP
Serve this dish immediately for maximum crunchiness, otherwise the grated carrots and apples will go limp.

Grated carrot and alfalfa sprout salad: Energy 194Kcal/818kJ; Protein 3g; Carbohydrate 41g, of which sugars 39g; Fat 3g; of which saturates 0g; Cholesterol 0mg; Calcium 70mg; Fibre 6.6g; Sodium 36mg.

Watermelon and feta salad

The combination of sweet juicy watermelon with salty feta cheese is refreshing and, along with the seeds and olives, makes a wonderfully nutritious Mediterranean salad. The juice of the lycopene-rich watermelon serves as a light dressing, and the seeds and olives are full of essential fatty acids.

Serves 4

4 slices watermelon, chilled
130g/4½oz feta cheese, cubed
handful of mixed seeds, such as
  pumpkin, sunflower, hemp and
  flax seed, lightly toasted
10–15 black olives
1 frisée lettuce, core removed
sprinkling of olive oil and fresh
  thyme, to garnish

COOK'S TIP
The best olives for this recipe
are the plump black varieties,
such as kalamata, other shiny,
brined varieties or dry-cured
black olives.

1 Cut the rind off the watermelon and remove as many of the seeds as you can. The sweetest and juiciest part of the fruit is at the core, and so you may want to cut off any whiter flesh just under the skin.

2 Cut the flesh into triangular chunks. Mix together the watermelon, feta cheese, mixed seeds and black olives.

3 Cover and chill for 30 minutes in the refrigerator before serving on a bed of lettuce leaves. Garnish with a drizzle of olive oil and a sprinkling of fresh thyme.

Watermelon and feta salad: Energy 256kcal/1066kJ; Protein 7.7g; Carbohydrate 12.9g, of which sugars 11.6g; Fat 19.7g, of which saturates 6.2g; Cholesterol 23mg; Calcium 165mg; Fibre 1.4g; Sodium 616mg.

Pink grapefruit and avocado salad

Peppery rocket leaves and the zesty tang of citrus fruits complement the creamy avocado beautifully in this refreshing salad. The heart-healthy monounsaturated oils of the avocado in this supernutrient-rich dish join the lycopene-rich pink grapefruit.

Serves 4

2 pink grapefruits
2 ripe avocados
30ml/2 tbsp chilli oil
90g/3½oz rocket (arugula) leaves

1 Slice the top and bottom off one of the grapefruits, then cut off all of the peel and pith from around the side – the best way to do this is to cut down in wide strips.

2 Working over a small bowl to catch the juices, cut out the segments from between the membranes and place them in a separate bowl. Squeeze any juices remaining in the membranes into the bowl, then discard them. Repeat with the remaining grapefruit.

3 Halve, stone (pit) and peel the avocados. Slice and add to the grapefruit. Whisk a pinch of salt into the grapefruit juice, followed by the chilli oil.

4 Pile the rocket leaves on to four plates and top with the grapefruit segments and avocado slices. Pour over the dressing and toss gently with your fingers. Serve immediately.

COOK'S TIP
• Coat the avocado in the grapefruit juice dressing, to stop it from browning.
• For added carbohydrate, the salad is delicious with wholemeal pasta or quinoa. Sprinkle with finely chopped walnuts and snipped fresh chives.

Pink grapefruit and avocado salad: Energy 151kcal/625kJ; Protein 1.1g; Carbohydrate 5.6g, of which sugars 5.2g; Fat 13.9g, of which saturates 2.4g; Cholesterol 0mg; Calcium 24mg; Fibre 1.9g; Sodium 13mg.

Grilled leek and courgette salad

This salad makes a delicious summery appetizer or main course when served on a bed of crisp, sweet lettuce. Whenever possible, choose young tender leeks and retain as much of the green part as possible, as this is where the nutrients are concentrated.

4 Heat the grill (broiler). Brush the leeks and courgettes lightly with oil. Grill (broil) the leeks for 2–3 minutes on each side and the courgettes for about 5 minutes on each side.

5 Place the grilled leeks in a shallow dish, together with the courgettes.

6 Place the remaining oil in a small bowl and whisk in the lemon rind, 15ml/1 tbsp lemon juice, the garlic, chilli and a pinch of sugar, if using. Season with salt and black pepper.

Serves 6

12 slender, baby leeks
6 small courgettes (zucchini)
45ml/3 tbsp extra virgin olive oil, plus extra for brushing
finely shredded rind and juice of ½ lemon
1–2 garlic cloves, finely chopped
½ fresh red chilli, seeded and diced
pinch of caster (superfine) sugar (optional)
50g/2oz/ ½ cup black olives, stoned (pitted) and roughly chopped
30ml/2 tbsp chopped fresh mint
150g/5oz feta cheese, sliced or crumbled
salt and ground black pepper
fresh mint leaves, to garnish

1 Bring a pan of water to the boil. Add the leeks and cook gently for 2–3 minutes.

2 Drain the leeks, refresh under cold water, then squeeze out any excess water and leave to drain.

3 Cut the courgettes in half lengthways. Place in a colander, adding 5ml/1 tsp salt to the layers, and leave to drain for about 45 minutes. Rinse well under running water and pat dry thoroughly on a piece of kitchen paper.

SUPERFOOD TIP
Olives are rich in vitamins A and E as well as copper and calcium.

7 Pour the dressing over the leeks and courgettes. Stir in the olives and chopped mint, then set aside to marinate for a few hours, turning the vegetables once or twice.

8 If the salad has been marinating in the refrigerator, remove it 30 minutes before serving and bring back to room temperature. When ready to serve, mix in the crumbled feta cheese and garnish with several fresh mint leaves.

Leek and courgette salad: Energy 197kcal/812kJ; Protein 6.2g; Carbohydrate 3.4g, of which sugars 2.9g; Fat 17.6g, of which saturates 5.3g; Cholesterol 18mg; Calcium 140mg; Fibre 2.6g; Sodium 552mg.

Quinoa salad with mango

Quinoa is a delicious gluten-free alternative to couscous or bulgur wheat, and is a wholesome vegetable protein. This nutrient-rich grain is best combined with ingredients that have a more robust flavour, such as fresh herbs, chilli, fruit and nuts, all of which feature in this fabulous salad.

Serves 4

130g/4½ oz quinoa
1 mango
60ml/4 tbsp pine nuts
large handful fresh basil,
  roughly chopped
large handful fresh flat leaf
  parsley, roughly chopped
large handful fresh mint,
  roughly chopped
1 mild long fresh red chilli,
  seeded and chopped

For the dressing
15ml/1 tbsp lemon juice
15ml/1 tbsp extra virgin olive oil
salt and ground black pepper

1 Put the quinoa in a pan and cover with cold water. Season with salt and bring to the boil. Reduce the heat, cover the pan with a lid and simmer for 12 minutes, or until the quinoa is tender. Drain well.

2 Meanwhile, prepare the mango. Cut vertically down each side of the stone (pit). Taking the two large slices, cut the flesh into a criss-cross pattern down to (but not through) the skin.

COOK'S TIP
You can enrich the flavour of quinoa by cooking in chicken or vegetable stock.

3 Press each half inside out, then cut the mango cubes away from the skin.

4 Toast the pine nuts for a few minutes in a dry frying pan until golden, then remove from the heat.

5 Mix together the ingredients for the dressing and season well.

6 Put the cooked quinoa into a bowl and add the herbs and chilli. Pour the dressing into the bowl and mix lightly until combined. Season to taste.

7 Transfer to a bowl or four shallow dishes. Arrange the mango on top of the herby quinoa and sprinkle with the pine nuts.

Quinoa salad with mango: Energy 206kcal/857kJ; Protein 4.5g; Carbohydrate 23.1g, of which sugars 6.2g; Fat 11.2g, of which saturates 1g; Cholesterol 0mg; Calcium 62mg; Fibre 2.5g; Sodium 9mg.

Lentil salad with red onion and garlic

This delicious, fragrant lentil salad is a great Moroccan-style dish, which can be served warm or chilled. As well as being high in fibre, this dish is also rich in the organosulphur compounds from the red onion and garlic, which have anti-inflammatory properties.

Serves 4

45ml/3 tbsp olive oil
2 red onions, chopped
2 tomatoes, peeled, seeded and chopped
10ml/2 tsp ground turmeric
10ml/2 tsp ground cumin
175g/6oz/¾ cup brown or green lentils, picked over and rinsed
900ml/1½ pints/3¾ cups vegetable stock or water
4 garlic cloves, crushed
small bunch of fresh coriander (cilantro), finely chopped
salt and ground black pepper
1 lemon, cut into wedges, to serve

1 Heat 30ml/2 tbsp of the oil in a large pan or flameproof casserole and fry the onions until soft.

2 Add the tomatoes, turmeric and cumin, then stir in the lentils. Pour in the stock or water and bring to the boil, then reduce the heat and simmer until the lentils are tender and almost all the liquid has been absorbed.

3 In a separate pan, fry the garlic in the remaining oil until brown and frizzled. Toss the garlic into the lentils with the fresh coriander and season to taste. Serve warm or cold, with wedges of lemon for squeezing over.

SUPERFOOD TIP
The vitamin C from the lemon juice will help to improve absorption of iron from the lentils.

Lentil salad: Energy 266Kcal/1116kJ; Protein 12.5g; Carbohydrate 35.1g, of which sugars 9.2g; Fat 9.4g, of which saturates 1.4g; Cholesterol 0mg; Calcium 73mg; Fibre 4.8g; Sodium 29mg.

Spinach and roast garlic salad

Roasting garlic sweetens its flavour and tones down its pungency, while still retaining all its goodness. Using young raw spinach leaves ensures that you are retaining all the nutrients, and the lemon juice in the dressing will help you absorb more of the iron.

Serves 4

12 garlic cloves, unpeeled
60 ml/4 tbsp extra virgin olive oil
450g/1lb baby spinach leaves
50g/2oz/½ cup pine nuts,
  lightly toasted
juice of ½ lemon
salt and freshly ground black
  pepper

COOK'S TIP
If spinach is to be served raw in a salad, the leaves need to be young and tender. Wash them well, drain and pat dry with absorbent paper.

1 Preheat the oven to 190°C/375°F/ Gas 5. Place the garlic in a small roasting dish, toss in 30ml/2 tbsp of the olive oil and bake for about 15 minutes, until the garlic cloves are slightly charred around the edges.

2 While still warm, transfer the garlic to a salad bowl. Add the spinach, pine nuts, lemon juice, remaining olive oil and a little salt. Toss well and add black pepper to taste. Serve immediately, inviting guests to squeeze the softened garlic purée out of the skin to eat.

Spinach and roast garlic salad: Energy 234Kcal/966kJ; Protein 6.1g; Carbohydrate 6g, of which sugars 3.7g; Fat 20.8g, of which saturates 2.3g; Cholesterol 0mg; Calcium 240mg; Fibre 4.6g; Sodium 23mg.

Orange, tomato and chive salsa

Both bursting with vitamin C, the orange and tomato make a cheerful combination of flavours lifted by the fragrant chopped chives and garlic. Its citrus zing makes this salsa perfect to serve with oily fish such as grilled (broiled) tuna steak or barbecued sardines.

2 Hold the orange in one hand over a bowl. Slice toward the middle of the fruit, to one side of a segment, and then gently twist the knife to ease the segment away from the membrane and out of the orange. Repeat to remove all the segments. Squeeze any juice from the remaining membrane. Prepare the second orange in the same way.

3 Roughly chop the orange segments and place them in the bowl with the collected juice.

4 Halve the tomato and use a teaspoon to scoop the seeds into the bowl. Finely dice the flesh and add to the oranges in the bowl.

5 Hold the bunch of chives neatly together and use a pair of kitchen scissors to snip them into the bowl.

Serves 4

2 large oranges
1 beefsteak tomato
a bunch of chives
1 garlic clove
30ml/2 tbsp olive oil
sea salt

VARIATION
Try adding a little diced mozzarella cheese to make a more substantial salsa.

1 Slice the top and bottom off the orange so that it will stand firmly on a chopping board. Using a large sharp knife, remove the peel by slicing from the top to the bottom of the orange.

6 Thinly slice the garlic and stir it into the orange mixture. Pour over the olive oil, season with sea salt and stir well to mix. Serve within 2 hours.

Orange, tomato and chive salsa: Energy 91Kcal/380kJ; Protein 1.3g; Carbohydrate 9.3g, of which sugars 9.3g; Fat 5.7g, of which saturates 0.8g; Cholesterol 0mg; Calcium 49mg; Fibre 2g; Sodium 7mg.

Black bean salsa

This salsa has a very striking appearance due to the black beans and bright red chillies. The beans are folate rich and this salsa is a great way to liven up any meal. Leave the salsa for a day or two after making, to allow the flavours to develop fully.

Serves 4 as an accompaniment

130g/4½oz/generous ½ cup black
  beans, soaked overnight in
  water to cover
1 dried red chilli
2 fresh red chillies
1 red onion
grated rind and juice of 1 lime
30ml/2 tbsp Mexican beer
  (optional)
15ml/1 tbsp olive oil
small bunch of fresh coriander
  (cilantro), chopped
salt

1 Drain the beans and put them in a large pan. Pour in water to cover and place the lid on the pan.

2 Bring to the boil, lower the heat slightly and simmer the beans for about 40 minutes, or until they are tender. They should still have a little bite and should not have begun to disintegrate.

3 Drain, rinse under cold water, then drain again and set the beans aside until they are cold.

4 Soak the dried red chilli in hot water for about 10 minutes, until softened. Wearing gloves if you prefer, drain, remove the stalk and then slit the chilli and scrape out the seeds with a small sharp knife. Chop the flesh finely.

5 Dry-fry the fresh red chillies in a griddle pan until the skins are scorched. Alternatively, spear them on a long-handled metal skewer and roast over the flame of a gas burner until the skins blister and darken. Don't let the flesh burn. Place the roasted chillies in a strong plastic bag and tie the top to keep the steam in. Set aside for 20 minutes.

6 Meanwhile, chop the red onion finely. Remove the chillies from the bag and peel off the skins. Slit them, remove the seeds and chop them finely.

7 Transfer the beans to a bowl and add the onion and both types of chilli. Stir in the lime rind and juice, the Mexican beer (if using), oil and coriander. Season with a little salt and mix well. Chill the salsa before serving.

> **COOK'S TIP**
> When preparing chillies, remember not to touch your eyes or face to avoid irritation.

Black bean salsa: Energy 126Kcal/533kJ; Protein 8.5g; Carbohydrate 15.8g, of which sugars 1.9g; Fat 3.5g, of which saturates 0.5g; Cholesterol 0mg; Calcium 48mg; Fibre 5.3g; Sodium 10mg.

Onion, mango and peanut chaat

Chaats are spiced relishes of vegetables and nuts served with Indian meals. This recipe combines the delightful sweet juiciness of mango with crunchy peanuts, both of which are bursting with an array of antioxidants. The fresh herbs add a fragrant aroma and flavour.

Serves 4

90g/3½ oz/scant 1 cup
  unsalted peanuts
15ml/1 tbsp peanut oil
1 onion, chopped
10cm/4in piece cucumber, seeded
  and cut into 5mm/¼ in dice
1 mango, peeled, stoned
  and diced
1 green chilli, seeded
  and chopped
30ml/2 tbsp chopped fresh
  coriander (cilantro)
15ml/1 tbsp chopped fresh mint
15ml/1 tbsp lime juice
pinch of light muscovado
  (brown) sugar

For the chaat masala
10ml/2 tsp ground toasted
  cumin seeds
2.5ml/½ tsp cayenne pepper
5ml/1 tsp mango powder (amchur)
2.5ml/½ tsp garam masala
pinch of ground asafoetida
salt and freshly ground
  black pepper

1 To make the chaat masala, grind all of the spices together, then season with 2.5ml/½ tsp each of salt and freshly ground black pepper.

2 Fry the peanuts in the oil until lightly browned, then drain them on kitchen paper until cool.

3 Mix the onion, cucumber, mango, chilli, fresh coriander and mint. Sprinkle in 5ml/1 tsp of the chaat masala. Stir in the peanuts and then add lime juice and/or sugar to taste. Set the mixture aside for 20–30 minutes for the flavours to mature.

4 Turn the mixture out into a serving bowl, sprinkle another 5ml/1 tsp of the chaat masala over and serve.

COOK'S TIP
Any remaining chaat masala will keep well in a sealed jar for 4–6 weeks.

VARIATION
Use other nuts such as cashews or almonds if you prefer not to use peanuts.

Onion, mango and peanut chaat: Energy 189Kcal/788kJ; Protein 6.9g; Carbohydrate 9.8g, of which sugars 6.6g; Fat 14g, of which saturates 2.4g; Cholesterol 0mg; Calcium 41mg; Fibre 2.4g; Sodium 4mg.

Brussels sprouts with chestnuts

When cooked correctly, the nutrient-packed Brussels sprout has a sweet flavour and a crunchy texture. This traditional recipe offers an inspiring way to eat this succulent vegetable. The sprouts blend wonderfully with the nutty flavour of the chestnuts and the slight saltiness of the bacon.

Serves 6

350g/12oz fresh chestnuts
300ml/½ pint/1¼ cups chicken or
   vegetable stock (optional)
   or water
5ml/1 tsp sugar
675g/1½lb Brussels sprouts
50g/2oz/4 tbsp butter
115g/4oz bacon, cut into strips

1 Cut a cross in the pointed end of each chestnut, then carefully place them in a pan of boiling water and cook for 5–10 minutes.

2 Drain the chestnuts and allow to cool before peeling off both the tough outer skin and the fine inner one of each chestnut.

3 Return the chestnuts to the pan, add the chicken or vegetable stock (if using) or water and sugar, and simmer gently for 30–35 minutes, until the chestnuts are tender, then drain thoroughly.

4 Meanwhile, cook the sprouts in lightly salted boiling water for 8–10 minutes, until just tender. Drain well and set aside.

5 Melt the butter, add the bacon, cook until it becomes crisp, then stir in the chestnuts for 2–3 minutes. Add the hot Brussels sprouts, toss together and serve.

SUPERFOOD TIP
Do not boil the Brussels sprouts for more than ten minutes, as this will destroy the sulphurous compounds which are thought to destroy pre-cancerous cells.

Brussels sprouts with chestnuts: Energy 256kcal/1070kJ; Protein 8.3g; Carbohydrate 26g, of which sugars 7.6g; Fat 13.9g, of which saturates 6.6g; Cholesterol 30mg; Calcium 59mg; Fibre 7g; Sodium 364mg.

Braised red cabbage

Red cabbage is sweeter-tasting than the green and white varieties, and combines well with fruit such as apples or raisins. The spices in this recipe enhance its sweetness, and braised red cabbage makes a wonderful accompaniment to roast pork, duck and game dishes.

Serves 4–6

1kg/2¼lb red cabbage
2 cooking apples
2 onions, chopped
5ml/1 tsp freshly grated nutmeg
1.5ml/¼ tsp ground cloves
1.5ml/¼ tsp ground cinnamon
15ml/1 tbsp soft dark brown sugar
45ml/3 tbsp red wine vinegar
25g/1oz/2 tbsp butter, diced
salt and ground black pepper
chopped flat leaf parsley,
   to garnish

1 Preheat the oven to 160°C/325°F/ Gas 3. Cut away and discard the large white ribs from the outer cabbage leaves using a large, sharp knife, then finely shred the cabbage. Peel, core and coarsely grate the apples.

2 Layer the shredded cabbage in a large ovenproof dish with the onions, apples, spices, sugar, and salt and ground black pepper. Pour over the vinegar and add the diced butter.

SUPERFOOD TIP
Cabbage is rich in vitamins A, C, B₆ and K, and is high in fibre.

3 Cover the dish with a lid and bake for about 1½ hours, stirring a couple of times, until the cabbage becomes very tender. Serve immediately, garnished with the parsley.

COOK'S TIP
Baking in a little liquid ensures that valuable nutrients are retained.

Braised red cabbage: Energy 160kcal/668kJ; Protein 4.3g; Carbohydrate 23.8g, of which sugars 22.4g; Fat 5.8g, of which saturates 3.3g; Cholesterol 13mg; Calcium 140mg; Fibre 6.6g; Sodium 58mg.

Kale with mustard dressing

The antioxidant-rich kale is an attractive vegetable with its dark green, curly leaves. Lightly steaming helps to retains the valuable vitamins, and the mustard dressing complements the slightly peppery flavour of the kale perfectly.

Serves 4

250g/9oz curly kale
45ml/3 tbsp light olive oil
5ml/1 tsp wholegrain mustard
15ml/1 tbsp white wine vinegar
pinch of caster (superfine) sugar
salt and ground black pepper

1 Wash the curly kale and drain it thoroughly. Trim the leaves and cut each one in two. Steam the kale for a few minutes to wilt the leaves then drain and set aside.

2 Whisk the oil into the mustard in a bowl. When it is blended completely, whisk in the white wine vinegar. The dressing should begin to thicken.

3 Season the mustard dressing to taste with sugar, salt and ground black pepper. Toss the kale in the dressing and serve immediately.

Kale with mustard dressing: Energy 99kcal/409kJ; Protein 2.1g; Carbohydrate 1.9g, of which sugars 1.9g; Fat 9.3g, of which saturates 1.3g; Cholesterol 0mg; Calcium 82mg; Fibre 2g; Sodium 27mg.

Braised Swiss chard

Braising Swiss chard in a small amount of water retains its impressive array of antioxidants and vitamins. Swiss chard can be used to make two tasty meals: on the first day, cook the leaves only; on the second day you can use the stalks by cooking them in the same way as asparagus.

Serves 4

900g/2lb Swiss chard or spinach
15g/½oz/1 tbsp butter
a little freshly grated nutmeg
sea salt and ground black pepper

COOK'S TIP
To cook Swiss chard stalks, trim the bases, wash them well and tie in bundles. Add to a pan of boiling water with a squeeze of lemon juice, and cook for about 20 minutes, or until tender but still slightly crisp. Drain and serve with a white sauce or pour over 30ml/ 2 tbsp fresh single (light) cream. Heat gently, season and serve.

1 Remove the stalks from the Swiss chard or spinach (and reserve the chard stalks, if you like – *see* Cook's Tip).

2 Wash the leaves well and lift straight into a lightly greased heavy pan; the water clinging to the leaves will be all that is needed for cooking process.

3 Cover with a tight-fitting lid and cook over a medium heat for about 3–5 minutes, or until just tender, shaking the pan occasionally.

4 Drain well, then add the butter and nutmeg, and season to taste. When the butter has melted, toss it into the cooked Swiss chard and leaves, and serve immediately.

Braised swiss chard: Energy 84Kcal/347kJ; Protein 6.3g; Carbohydrate 3.6g, of which sugars 3.4g; Fat 4.9g, of which saturates 2.2g; Cholesterol 8mg; Calcium 383mg; Fibre 4.7g; Sodium 338mg.

Roast beetroot with horseradish cream

The sweet flavour of the vibrant pink beetroot is enhanced first by roasting and then by the nutrient-rich, cruciferous horseradish and vinegar. Opt for small and tender beets to enjoy the best of this high-fibre vitamin- and mineral-rich vegetable.

Serves 4–6

10–12 small whole beetroots (beets)
30ml/2 tbsp oil
45ml/3 tbsp grated fresh
  horseradish
15ml/1 tbsp white wine vinegar
10ml/2 tsp caster (superfine) sugar
150ml/¼ pint/⅔ cup double
  (heavy) cream
salt

COOK'S TIPS
• If you are unable to find fresh horseradish root, use preserved grated horseradish instead.
• For a lighter sauce, replace half of the cream with thick natural (plain) yogurt or crème fraîche.

1 Preheat the oven to 180°C/350°F/ Gas 4. Wash the beetroots without breaking their skins. Trim the stalks but do not remove them completely.

2 Toss the beetroot in the oil and sprinkle with salt. Spread them in a roasting pan and cover with foil. Put into the oven and cook for about 1½ hours, or until soft throughout. Leave to cool, covered, for 10 minutes.

3 Meanwhile, make the horseradish sauce. Put the horseradish, vinegar and sugar into a bowl and mix well. Whip the cream until thickened and fold in the horseradish mixture. Cover and chill until required.

4 When the beetroots are cool enough to handle, gently slip off the skins and serve them with the horseradish sauce.

Roast beetroot: Energy 254kcal/1052kJ; Protein 2.1g; Carbohydrate 10g, of which sugars 9.1g; Fat 22.2g, of which saturates 3.2g; Cholesterol 1mg; Calcium 26mg; Fibre 2.3g; Sodium 143mg.

Carrot and parsnip purée

Antioxidant and vitamin A-rich carrots are blended with creamy vitamin C- and vitamin K-rich parsnips. These two root vegetables work especially well together and are often found in a soup, or in this popular warm and comforting side dish.

Serves 6–8

350g/12oz carrots
450g/1lb parsnips
pinch of freshly grated nutmeg
   or ground mace
15g/½oz/1 tbsp butter
15ml/1 tbsp single (light) cream,
   or top of the milk (optional)
1 small bunch parsley leaves,
   chopped (optional), plus extra
   to garnish
salt and ground black pepper

1 Peel the carrots and slice thinly. Peel the parsnips and cut into bitesize chunks (they are softer and will cook more quickly than the carrots). Boil the two vegetables, separately, in salted water, until tender.

2 Drain them well and put them through a *mouli-légumes* (food mill) with the grated nutmeg or mace, a good seasoning of salt and ground black pepper, and the butter. Purée together and check for seasoning.

COOK'S TIP
Leftover purée can be thinned to taste with quality chicken stock for a quick home-made soup.

3 If you like, blend in some cream or top of the milk to taste, and add chopped parsley for extra flavour. Transfer the purée to a warmed serving bowl, sprinkle with freshly chopped parsley to garnish and serve.

Carrot purée: Energy 92Kcal/385kJ; Protein 1.8g; Carbohydrate 14.1g, of which sugars 8.7g; Fat 3.5g, of which saturates 1.8g; Cholesterol 7mg; Calcium 48mg; Fibre 4.9g; Sodium 38mg.

Roasted Jerusalem artichokes

High in iron and potassium, Jerusalem artichokes conceal a deliciously sweet, nutty white flesh inside their knobbly brown exterior. While they are most popularly used for making creamy soups, they also taste fabulous roasted or puréed and served as a side vegetable to many foods.

Serves 6

675g/1½lb Jerusalem artichokes
15ml/1 tbsp lemon juice or vinegar
salt
50g/2oz/¼ cup unsalted butter
seasoned flour, for dusting

1 Peel the artichokes, dropping them immediately into a bowl of water acidulated with lemon juice or vinegar to prevent browning.

2 Cut up the artichokes into equal sized pieces, otherwise they will cook unevenly.

3 Preheat the oven to 180°C/350°F/ Gas 4. Drain the artichokes from the acidulated water. Bring a pan of salted water to the boil.

4 Boil the drained artichokes for 5 minutes, or until just tender. Watch them carefully, as they break up easily.

5 Melt the butter in a roasting pan, coat the artichokes in the seasoned flour and roll them around in the butter in the pan.

6 Roast the butter- and flour-coated artichokes in the preheated oven for 20–30 minutes, or until golden brown. Serve immediately.

VARIATION
Puréeing is a useful fall-back if the artichokes break up during cooking: simply blend or mash the drained boiled artichokes with salt and freshly ground black pepper to taste, and a little single (light) cream, if you like.

Artichokes: Energy 101Kcal/419kJ; Protein 0.7g; Carbohydrate 8.9g, of which sugars 8.4g; Fat 7.2g, of which saturates 4.5g; Cholesterol 18mg; Calcium 30mg; Fibre 2.7g; Sodium 242mg.

Split pea and shallot mash

Ring the changes with this excellent alternative to mashed potatoes. This hearty side dish is rich in nutrients and will count toward one of your five-a-day fruit and vegetables. Split peas are delicious when puréed with shallots and enlivened with cumin seeds and fresh herbs.

Serves 4–6

225g/8oz/1 cup yellow split peas
1 bay leaf
8 sage leaves, roughly chopped
15ml/1 tbsp olive oil
3 shallots, finely chopped
8ml/heaped 1 tsp cumin seeds
1 large garlic clove, chopped
50g/2oz/4 tbsp butter, softened
salt and freshly ground
    black pepper

SUPERFOOD TIPS
• Like other pulses, split peas are an excellent source of protein, fibre, minerals and B vitamins.
• Split peas are particularly good for diabetics, as they can help to control blood sugar levels.

1 Place the split peas in a bowl and cover with cold water. Leave to soak overnight, then rinse and drain.

2 Place the drained split peas in a pan, cover with fresh cold water and bring to the boil. Skim off any foam that rises to the surface, then reduce the heat.

3 Add the bay leaf and sage, and simmer for 30–40 minutes, until the peas are tender. Add more water during cooking, if necessary.

4 Meanwhile, heat the oil in a frying pan and cook the shallots, cumin seeds and garlic over a medium heat for 3 minutes, or until the shallots soften, stirring occasionally. Add the mixture to the split peas while they are still cooking.

5 Drain the split peas, reserving the cooking water. Remove the bay leaf, then place the split peas in a food processor or blender with the butter and season well.

6 Add 105ml/7 tbsp of the reserved cooking water and blend until the mixture forms a coarse purée. Add more water if the mash seems to be too dry. Adjust the seasoning and serve warm.

Split pea and shallot mash: Energy 201Kcal/845kJ; Protein 9.1g; Carbohydrate 22g, of which sugars 1.5g; Fat 9.2g, of which saturates 4.7g; Cholesterol 18mg; Calcium 23mg; Fibre 2g; Sodium 64mg.

Cauliflower with egg and lemon

Cauliflower is as good as broccoli on the nutritional front, and boiling it lightly retains this goodness. Serving with a sauce is very traditional, and this delicious light, zingy lemon sauce is not too rich, and is also made without wheat flour.

**Serves 4 as a main course,
6 as a starter**

75–90ml/5–6 tbsp extra virgin
   olive oil
1 medium cauliflower, divided
   into large florets
2 eggs
juice of 1 lemon
5ml/1 tsp cornflour (cornstarch),
   mixed to a cream with a little
   cold water
30ml/2 tbsp chopped fresh flat
   leaf parsley
salt

VARIATION
Replace the cauliflower with broccoli or combine both for a more colourful option.

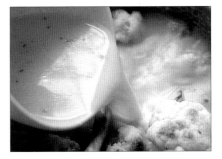

1 Heat the olive oil in a large heavy pan, add the cauliflower florets and sauté over a medium heat until they start to brown.

2 Pour in enough hot water to almost cover the cauliflower, add salt to taste, then cover the pan and cook for 7–8 minutes, until the florets are just soft. Remove the pan from the heat and leave to stand, covered, while you make the sauce.

3 Beat the eggs in a bowl, add the lemon juice and cornflour and beat until well mixed. Now, beat in a few tablespoons of the hot liquid from the cauliflower. Pour the egg mixture over the cauliflower, then stir gently.

4 Place the pan over a very gentle heat for 2 minutes to thicken the sauce. Spoon into a warmed serving bowl, sprinkle the chopped parsley over the top and serve.

Cauliflower with egg and lemon: Energy 210Kcal/833kJ; Protein 7g; Carbohydrate 4.4g, of which sugars 2.7g; Fat 17.5g, of which saturates 3g; Cholesterol 95mg; Calcium 51mg; Fibre 2.2g; Sodium 47mg.

Chilli rice with turmeric and coriander

This is a lively rice accompaniment which is packed full of flavour, colour and heat. The chillies stimulate the body and the addition of turmeric helps to enrich its antioxidant goodness. Using brown rice adds to the nutrient content and also improves its glycaemic index.

Serves 4

15ml/1 tbsp vegetable oil or sesame oil
2–3 green or red Thai chillies, seeded and finely chopped
2 garlic cloves, finely chopped
2.5cm/1in fresh root ginger, finely chopped
5ml/1 tsp sugar
10–15ml/2 tsp–1 tbsp ground turmeric
225g/8oz/generous 1 cup long grain brown rice
30ml/2 tbsp fish sauce
600ml/1 pint/2½ cups water, or fish, vegetable or chicken stock
a bunch of fresh coriander (cilantro) leaves, finely chopped
salt and ground black pepper

1 Heat the oil in a heavy pan. Stir in the chillies, garlic and ginger with the sugar. As they begin to colour, stir in the turmeric.

2 Add the rice, coating it in the turmeric and flavourings, then pour in the fish sauce and the water or stock – the liquid should sit about 2.5cm/1in above the rice.

3 Season with salt and pepper and bring the liquid to the boil. Reduce the heat, cover and simmer for about 25 minutes, or until the water has been absorbed.

4 Remove the pan from the heat and leave the rice to steam for a further 10 minutes.

5 Pour the rice on to a serving dish. Add some of the coriander and lightly toss together using a fork. Garnish with the remaining coriander.

COOK'S TIP
Take care when chopping chillies as they can cause irritation to the skin and eyes.

Chilli rice with turmeric: Energy 252Kcal/1066kJ; Protein 5g; Carbohydrate 51g, of which sugars 1g; Fat 5g, of which saturates 1g; Cholesterol 0mg; Calcium 24mg; Fibre 0.3g; Sodium 0.5g.

Layered herring salad

This traditional Russian salad looks like a layered cake. A colourful range of nutrient-rich fruit and vegetables together with mayonnaise joins the omega 3-rich herring fillets. This dish is always topped with a layer of grated hard-boiled eggs, boosting your vitamin A, B and D intake.

**Serves 8 as an appetizer,
 4 as a main course**

250g/9oz salted herring fillets
3 carrots, total weight 250g/9oz
4 eggs
1 small red onion
200g/7oz/scant 1 cup mayonnaise
5–6 cooked beetroots (beets),
 total weight 300g/11oz
2 eating apples
45ml/3 tbsp chopped fresh dill,
 to garnish

1 Soak the herring in water overnight. The next day, rinse them under running water and then drain. Cut into small pieces and put in a bowl.

2 Put the whole carrots in a pan of cold water, bring to the boil, then reduce the heat, cover and simmer for 10–15 minutes, until just tender. Drain and put under cold running water. Set aside.

3 Meanwhile, put the eggs in a pan, cover with cold water and bring to the boil. Reduce the heat and simmer for 10 minutes. When the eggs are cooked, drain immediately and put under cold running water. Set aside.

4 Finely chop the onion and add to the herrings with 15ml/1 tbsp of the mayonnaise. Spread the mixture over a 25cm/10in serving plate.

5 Coarsely grate the carrots, beetroots and apples into small piles. Add a layer of grated beetroot over the herring mixture and spread 45–60ml/ 3–4 tbsp mayonnaise on top. Repeat with a layer of grated carrots and mayonnaise, then a layer of apple.

6 Finally spread a thin layer of mayonnaise over the top of the salad. Cover with clear film (plastic wrap) and chill in the refrigerator for at least 1 hour or overnight.

7 Just before serving, remove the shell from the eggs and grate coarsely. Sprinkle the grated egg all over the salad so that it is covered completely and creates a final layer, then garnish with chopped dill.

VARIATION
Use pickled beetroot for an added tang of vinegar.

Layered herring salad: Energy 130kcal/544kJ; Protein 12.1g; Carbohydrate 9.3g, of which sugars 8.7g; Fat 5.3g, of which saturates 0.8g; Cholesterol 95mg; Calcium 96mg; Fibre 2.2g; Sodium 1697mg.

Marinated salmon with avocado

Use only the freshest of salmon for this salad, as the marinade of lemon and dashi-konbu 'cooks' the omega 3-rich salmon. Serving with avocado, toasted almonds, salad leaves and the miso mayonnaise makes this an interesting Mediterranean and Japanese fusion of flavours.

Serves 4

250g/9oz very fresh salmon tail, skinned and filleted
juice of 1 lemon
10cm/4in dashi-konbu (dried kelp), wiped with a damp cloth and cut into 4 strips
1 ripe avocado
4 shiso leaves, stalks removed and cut in half lengthways
about 115g/4oz mixed leaves such as lamb's lettuce, frisée or rocket (arugula)
45ml/3 tbsp flaked (sliced) almonds, toasted in a dry frying pan until just slightly browned

For the miso mayonnaise
90ml/6 tbsp good-quality mayonnaise
15ml/1 tbsp shiromiso (white miso)
ground black pepper

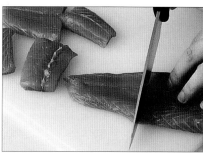

1 Cut the first salmon fillet in half crossways at the tail end where the fillet is not wider than 4cm/1½in. Now, cut the wider part in half lengthways. Cut the other fillet into three pieces, in the same way.

2 Pour the lemon juice and two of the dashi-konbu pieces into a wide, shallow plastic container. Lay the salmon fillets in the base and sprinkle with the rest of the dashi-konbu.

3 Marinate for about 15 minutes, then turn once and leave for a further 15 minutes. The salmon should turn a pink 'cooked' colour.

4 Remove the salmon from the marinade and wipe with kitchen paper. Now, cut the salmon into 5mm/¼in thick slices against the grain.

5 Halve the avocado and sprinkle with a little of the salmon marinade. Remove the avocado stone (pit) and skin, then carefully slice to the same thickness as the salmon.

6 Mix the miso mayonnaise ingredients in a bowl. Spread about 5ml/1 tsp on to the back of each of the shiso leaves. Mix the remainder with 15ml/1 tbsp of the remaining marinade to loosen the mayonnaise.

7 Arrange the salad leaves on four plates. Top with the avocado, salmon, shiso leaves and almonds, and drizzle over the remaining miso mayonnaise.

8 Alternatively, build a tower of avocado and salmon slices by putting an eighth of the avocado slices in the centre of a plate, slightly overlapping. Add a shiso leaf, miso-side down, and top with salmon slices.

9 Repeat the process. Arrange the salad leaves and almonds, spoon over the miso mayonnaise and serve.

Salmon with avocado: Energy 432kcal/1787kJ; Protein 16.2g; Carbohydrate 2.3g, of which sugars 1.4g; Fat 39.8g, of which saturates 6.2g; Cholesterol 48mg; Calcium 54mg; Fibre 2.3g; Sodium 134mg.

Citrus chicken coleslaw

This zesty coleslaw salad makes a refreshing change from the rich mayonnaise version, its crisp shredded vegetables combining well with the protein-rich chicken and the lovely citrus dressing. Use leftover Christmas turkey for a fabulous seasonal buffet dish.

Serves 6

120ml/4fl oz/½ cup extra virgin olive oil
6 boneless chicken breasts, skinned
4 oranges
5ml/1 tsp Dijon mustard
15ml/1 tbsp clear honey
300g/11oz/2¾ cups white cabbage, finely shredded
300g/11oz carrots, peeled and finely sliced
2 spring onions (scallions), sliced
2 celery sticks, cut into matchstick strips
30ml/2 tbsp fresh tarragon, chopped
2 limes
salt and ground black pepper

1 Heat 30ml/2 tbsp of the oil in a large, heavy frying pan. Add the chicken breasts to the pan and cook for 15–20 minutes, or until the chicken is cooked through and golden brown. (If your pan is too small, cook the chicken in two or three batches.) Remove the chicken from the pan and leave to cool.

VARIATION
For a creamy result, mayonnaise, crème fraîche or sour cream can be used to dress the chicken instead of the orange, oil and honey mixture.

2 Peel two of the oranges, cutting off all the pith, then separate the segments and set aside. Grate the rind and squeeze the juice from one of the remaining oranges and place in a large bowl.

3 Stir in the Dijon mustard, 5ml/ 1 tsp of the honey, 60ml/4 tbsp of the oil, and season to taste. Mix in the cabbage, carrots, spring onions and celery. Leave to stand for 10 minutes.

4 Meanwhile, squeeze the juice from the rest of the orange and mix it with the remaining honey and oil and the tarragon. Peel and segment the limes and lightly mix them into the dressing with the reserved orange segments. Season to taste.

5 Slice the cooked chicken breasts and stir into the dressing. Spoon the vegetable salad on to plates and add the chicken mixture. Serve at once.

Citrus chicken coleslaw: Energy 293kcal/1219kJ; Protein 21g; Carbohydrate 5g, of which sugars 5g; Fat 21g, of which saturates 3g; Cholesterol 58mg; Calcium 37mg; Fibre 1.4g; Sodium 165mg.

Thai beef salad

Try to buy lean grass-fed beef if possible for this dish and cut off any excess fat. This iron-rich dish is full of flavours and textures that will liven up any lunch. Shiitake mushrooms, garlic and chillies add to the superfood count, as does serving with a crisp salad to make a delicious lunch.

Serves 4

675g/1½lb fillet or rump steak
30ml/2 tbsp olive oil
2 small mild red chillies, seeded
    and sliced
225g/8oz/3¼ cups shiitake
    mushrooms, sliced

For the dressing
3 spring onions (scallions), finely
    chopped
2 garlic cloves, finely chopped
juice of 1 lime
15–30ml/1–2 tbsp fish or oyster
    sauce, to taste
5ml/1 tsp soft light brown sugar
30ml/2 tbsp chopped fresh
    coriander (cilantro)

To serve
1 cos or romaine lettuce, torn
    into strips
175g/6oz cherry tomatoes, halved
5cm/2in piece cucumber, peeled,
    halved and thinly sliced
45ml/3 tbsp toasted sesame seeds

1 Preheat the grill until hot, then cook the steak for 2–4 minutes on each side, depending on how well done you like steak. (In Thailand, the beef is traditionally served quite rare.) Leave to cool for at least 15 minutes.

2 Use a very sharp knife to slice the meat as thinly as possible, and place the slices in a bowl.

3 Heat the olive oil in a frying pan. Add the seeded and sliced red chillies and the sliced mushrooms, and cook for 5 minutes, stirring occasionally.

4 Turn off the heat and add the grilled steak slices to the pan. Stir well to coat the beef slices in the chilli and mushroom mix.

5 Stir all the ingredients for the dressing together, then pour it over the meat mixture and toss gently.

6 Arrange the cos or romaine lettuce, tomatoes and cucumber slices on a serving plate. Spoon the warm steak mixture in the centre and sprinkle the sesame seeds over. Serve immediately.

Thai beef salad: Energy 381Kcal/1591kJ; Protein 39.8g; Carbohydrate 4.1g, of which sugars 3.8g; Fat 23g, of which saturates 6.6g; Cholesterol 103mg; Calcium 105mg; Fibre 2.5g; Sodium 352mg.

Mayonnaise

Using a combination of these omega 3-rich oils makes this a healthier mayonnaise option. Use it to make coleslaw or potato salad, or flavour it with a pesto or garlic sauce, known as aioli. It still has the same calories and fat, so remember to use it sparingly.

Makes 300ml/½ pint/1¼ cups

250ml/ 8 fl oz/1 cup rapeseed oil
50ml/2 fl oz/¼ cup flaxseed oil
1 egg
15ml/1 tbsp white wine vinegar
10ml/2 tsp smooth mustard
   (English or French)

Aioli
2 crushed garlic cloves
15ml/1 tbsp lemon juice
Salt and pepper

1 Mix the rapeseed and flaxseed oils together in a jug (pitcher).

2 Place the egg, vinegar and mustard of your choice into the liquidizer and mix well for a few seconds.

3 With the liquidizer on, pour a thin stream of oil gradually into the egg mix. The mayonnaise will start to thicken when about two-thirds of the oil has been added; a little patience may be useful at this stage!

WARNING
As this mayonnaise contains raw egg, it should be avoided by pregnant women, and the very young and old.

4 Incorporate the remaining oil into the thickened mayonnaise by stirring, if you find that the liquidizer can no longer blend the mixture fully.

5 If flavouring the mayonnaise with aioli, blend in the garlic cloves, lemon juice and seasoning.

Omega-3-rich salad dressing

Add fresh green herbs of your choice, depending on what you are serving your salad with. Add dill for fish, thyme and parsley if serving with chicken. Flaxseed oil can have a strong flavour, so combining it with the rapeseed oil tones this down a little.

Makes 120ml/4fl oz

40mls/3 tbsp sherry vinegar
40mls/3 tbsp rapeseed oil
40mls/3 tbsp flaxseed oil
30ml/2 tbsp handful of chopped
   fresh herbs such as parsley,
   chives and coriander (cilantro)
2.5ml/½ tsp coarse mustard
fresh ground black pepper

1 Place all of the ingredients in a screw-top jar or bottle, and shake up and down vigorously until well mixed. Drizzle the dressing over the salad of your choice.

Mayonnaise: Energy 2809Kcal/11588kJ; Protein 9g; Carbohydrate 3g, of which sugars 2g; Fat 308g, of which saturates 23g; Cholesterol 238mg; Calcium 48mg; Fibre 0.3g: Sodium 599mg.
Omega 3 dressing: Energy 734Kcal/3042kJ; Protein 1g; Carbohydrate 1g, of which sugars 1g; Fat 81g, of which saturates 6g; Cholesterol 0mg; Calcium 18mg; Fibre 0.6g; Sodium 117mg.

MAIN DISHES

Tempting, yet nutritionally balanced main dishes can be made from a huge variety of healthy ingredients, from lean poultry, oily fish and eggs to nuts, pulses and grains. Not only are these recipes substantial, they are also packed with fibre, vitamins and minerals. The selection of hearty dishes in this chapter offers you the freedom to choose from a quick weekday supper, such as Red Pepper Risotto or Pea and Mint Omelette, to a more relaxed weekend dinner such as Beef Stew with Oysters, or Moroccan Lamb with Honey and Prunes.

Vegetable couscous with olives and almonds

This Mediterranean-style recipe includes the cardio-protective ingredients of olives, almonds and olive oil. Couscous is a light and fluffy ingredient that is low in fat and high in starchy carbohydrate. It is actually a wheat product, so for a gluten-free version, use quinoa or brown rice.

Serves 4

275g/10oz/1⅔ cups couscous
525ml/18fl oz/2¼ cups boiling
   vegetable stock
16–20 black olives
2 small courgettes (zucchini)
25g/1oz/¼cup flaked (sliced)
   almonds, toasted
60ml/4 tbsp olive oil
15ml/1 tbsp lemon juice
15ml/1 tbsp chopped fresh
   coriander (cilantro)
15ml/1 tbsp chopped fresh parsley
good pinch of ground cumin
good pinch of paprika

1 Place the couscous in a heatproof bowl and pour over the boiling vegetable stock. Stir with a fork to combine, then set aside for 10 minutes. When the stock has been absorbed, fluff the grains with a fork.

2 Meanwhile, halve the olives and discard the stones (pits). Trim the courgettes and cut them into matchsticks.

3 Add the courgette strips, black olives and toasted almonds to the bowl of couscous and gently mix together to combine thoroughly.

4 Blend together the olive oil, lemon juice, herbs and spices. Pour the dressing over the couscous. Gently stir to combine, and serve.

VARIATIONS
• Add extra flavour to this salad by stirring in 10ml/2 tsp grated fresh root ginger.
• Vary the flavour of this dish with alternative combinations of vegetables such as chopped tomatoes, cucumber matchsticks, diced roatsted pumpkin or diced cooked aubergine.

Vegetable couscous: Energy 319Kcal/1326kJ; Protein 6.6g; Carbohydrate 36.9g, of which sugars 1.4g; Fat 16.9g, of which saturates 2.1g; Cholesterol 0mg; Calcium 73mg; Fibre 1.9g; Sodium 287mg.

Roasted ratatouille moussaka

Roasting this colourful rainbow of vegetables in olive oil and garlic intensifies the rich flavours, contrasting with the light and mouthwatering egg-and-cheese topping. Make one large dish to share or divide the roasted vegetables and topping among individual gratin dishes.

Serves 4–6

2 red (bell) peppers, seeded and
   cut into large chunks
2 yellow (bell) peppers, seeded
   and cut into large chunks
2 aubergines (eggplant), cut into
   large chunks
3 courgettes (zucchini), sliced
45ml/3 tbsp olive oil
3 garlic cloves, crushed
400g/14oz can chopped tomatoes
30ml/2 tbsp sun-dried tomato paste
45ml/3 tbsp chopped fresh basil or
   15ml/1 tbsp dried basil
15ml/1 tbsp balsamic vinegar
1.5ml/¼ tsp soft light brown sugar
salt and fresh ground black pepper
basil leaves, to garnish

For the topping
25g/1oz/2 tbsp butter
25g/1oz/¼ cup plain
   (all-purpose) flour
300ml/½ pint/1¼ cups milk
1.5ml/¼ tsp freshly grated nutmeg
250g/9oz ricotta cheese
3 eggs, beaten
25g/1oz/⅓ cup freshly grated
   Parmesan cheese

1 Preheat the oven to 230°C/450°F/ Gas 8. Arrange the peppers, aubergines and courgettes in a large roasting tin (pan). Season well.

2 Mix together the oil and crushed garlic and pour over the vegetables.

3 Roast in the oven for 15–20 minutes, until slightly charred, lightly tossing the vegetables once during cooking time. Remove the tin (pan) from the oven and set aside. Reduce the oven temperature to 200°C/400°F/Gas 6.

4 Put the chopped tomatoes, tomato paste, basil, balsamic vinegar and brown sugar in a pan and heat to boiling point. Simmer for 10–15 minutes until thickened, stirring occasionally. Season to taste.

5 Carefully tip the roasted vegetables into the pan of tomato sauce. Mix well, and spoon the vegetables into an ovenproof dish. Level the surface.

6 For the topping, melt the butter in a large pan over a gentle heat. Stir in the flour and cook for 1 minute. Pour in the milk, stirring constantly, then whisk until blended. Add the nutmeg and whisk until thickened. Cook for 2 more minutes.

7 Remove from the heat and allow to cool slightly. Mix in the ricotta cheese and beaten eggs. Season to taste.

8 Spoon the topping over the vegetables and sprinkle with the Parmesan cheese. Bake for 30–35 minutes until the topping is golden brown. Serve immediately, garnished with basil leaves.

Moussaka: Energy 570Kcal/2367kJ; Protein 22.1g; Carbohydrate 27.5g, of which sugars 21.7g; Fat 42.1g, of which saturates 20.3g; Cholesterol 223mg; Calcium 339mg; Fibre 7.1g; Sodium 447mg.

Mediterranean vegetable hot-pot

This dish epitomizes the essence of Mediterranean cuisine, which includes vegetables, pulses, olive oil and garlic. It's a one-dish meal that is suitable for feeding large numbers of people, so it is great for family gatherings. This tastes fabulous served with crusty, fresh bread and a crisp, green salad.

Serves 4

60ml/4 tbsp extra virgin olive oil
  or sunflower oil
1 large onion, chopped
2 small or medium aubergines
  (eggplants), cut into small cubes
4 courgettes (zucchini), cut into
  small chunks
2 red, yellow or green (bell)
  peppers, seeded and chopped
115g/4oz/1 cup fresh or frozen peas
115g/4oz green beans
200g/7oz can flageolet beans,
  rinsed and drained
450g/1lb new or salad potatoes,
  peeled and cubed
2.5ml/½ tsp ground cinnamon
2.5ml/½ tsp ground cumin
5ml/1 tsp paprika
4–5 tomatoes, peeled
400g/14oz can chopped tomatoes
30ml/2 tbsp chopped fresh parsley
3–4 garlic cloves, crushed
350ml/12fl oz/1½ cups
  vegetable stock
salt and ground black pepper
black olives and fresh parsley,
  to garnish

1 Preheat the oven to 190°C/375°F/ Gas 5. Heat 45ml/3 tbsp of the oil in a heavy pan, and cook the onion until golden. Add the aubergines, sauté for 3 minutes, then add the courgettes, peppers, peas, beans and potatoes. Stir in the spices and seasoning. Cook for 3 minutes, stirring constantly.

2 Cut the tomatoes in half and scoop out the seeds. Chop the tomatoes finely and place them in a bowl. Stir in the canned tomatoes with the chopped fresh parsley, crushed garlic and the remaining olive oil. Spoon the aubergine mixture into a shallow ovenproof dish and level the surface.

3 Pour the stock over the aubergine mixture and then spoon over the prepared tomato mixture.

4 Cover the dish with foil and bake for 30–45 minutes, until the vegetables are tender. Serve hot, garnished with black olives and parsley.

Mediterranean hot-pot: Energy 365kcal/1529kJ; Protein 14.3g; Carbohydrate 48.2g, of which sugars 20.1g; Fat 14.1g, of which saturates 2.3g; Cholesterol 0mg; Calcium 141mg; Fibre 12.8g; Sodium 224mg.

Barley risotto with roasted squash

Made with nutty-flavoured, slightly chewy pearl barley, this risotto is more like a pilaff than a classic Italian risotto, which is made with rice. Using barley improves the glycaemic index of this dish, so energy is released into the body nice and slowly.

Serves 4–5

200g/7oz/1 cup pearl barley
1 butternut squash, peeled, seeded and cut into chunks
10ml/2 tsp chopped fresh thyme
60ml/4 tbsp olive oil
25g/1oz/2 tbsp butter
4 leeks, cut into fairly thick diagonal slices
2 garlic cloves, finely chopped
175g/6oz brown cap (cremini) mushrooms, sliced
2 carrots, coarsely grated
about 120ml/4fl oz/½ cup vegetable stock
30ml/2 tbsp chopped fresh flat leaf parsley
50g/2oz Pecorino cheese, grated
45ml/3 tbsp pumpkin seeds, toasted, or chopped walnuts
salt and ground black pepper

1 Rinse the barley, then cook it in simmering water, keeping the pan part-covered, for 35–45 minutes, or until tender. Drain. Preheat the oven to 200°C/400°F/Gas 6.

2 Place the squash in a roasting pan with half the thyme. Season with pepper and toss with half the oil. Roast, stirring once, for 30–35 minutes, until tender and beginning to brown.

3 Heat half the butter with the remaining oil in a large pan. Cook the leeks and garlic gently for 5 minutes.

4 Add the mushrooms and remaining thyme, then cook until the liquid from the mushrooms evaporates and they begin to fry.

5 Stir in the carrots and cook for 2 minutes, then add the barley and most of the stock. Season well and part-cover the pan. Cook for another 5 minutes. Pour in the remaining stock if the mixture seems dry.

6 Stir in the parsley, the remaining butter and half the Pecorino, then stir in the squash. Add seasoning to taste and serve immediately, sprinkled with the toasted pumpkin seeds or walnuts and the remaining Pecorino.

Barley risotto: Energy 409kcal/1713kJ; Protein 11.8g; Carbohydrate 43.4g, of which sugars 7.1g; Fat 22.1g, of which saturates 6.6g; Cholesterol 21mg; Calcium 249mg; Fibre 4.9g; Sodium 159mg.

Red pepper risotto

Rich in vitamin C and carotenoids, which are all antioxidants, red and yellow peppers are far sweeter than the green varieties. Chargrilling intensifies this sweet flavour and makes for an excellent vegetarian supper dish or even an appetizer for six people.

Serves 4

1 red (bell) pepper
1 yellow (bell) pepper
15ml/1 tbsp olive oil
25g/1oz/2 tbsp butter
1 onion, chopped
2 garlic cloves, crushed
275g/10oz/1½ cups risotto rice
1 litre/1¾ pints/4 cups simmering
  vegetable stock
50g/2oz/⅔ cup freshly grated
  Parmesan cheese
salt and freshly ground
  black pepper
freshly grated Parmesan cheese,
  to serve (optional)

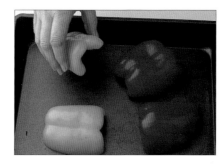

1 Preheat the grill (broiler) to high. Halve the peppers, remove the seeds and pith and place, cut-side down, on a baking sheet. Place under the grill for 5 minutes, until the skin is charred. Put the peppers in a plastic bag, tie the ends and leave for 4–5 minutes.

2 Peel the peppers when they are cool enough to handle and the steam has loosened the skin. Slice into thin strips.

3 Heat the oil and butter in a pan and fry the onion and garlic for 4–5 minutes over a low heat, until the onion begins to soften. Add the peppers and cook the mixture for 3–4 minutes more, stirring occasionally.

4 Stir in the rice. Cook over a medium heat for 3–4 minutes, stirring all the time, until the rice is evenly coated in oil and the outer part of each grain has become translucent.

5 Add a ladleful of stock. Cook, stirring, until all the liquid has been absorbed. Continue to add the stock, a ladleful at a time, making sure each quantity has been absorbed before adding the next.

6 When the rice is tender but retains a bit of 'bite', stir in the Parmesan, and season to taste. Cover and leave to stand for 3–4 minutes, then serve, with extra Parmesan, if using.

> **COOK'S TIP**
> Add a few strands of saffron to the stock for vibrant yellow rice.

Red pepper risotto: Energy 555Kcal/2312kJ; Protein 16.1g; Carbohydrate 80.1g, of which sugars 10g; Fat 18g, of which saturates 8.4g; Cholesterol 34mg; Calcium 238mg; Fibre 2.6g; Sodium 241mg.

Buckwheat with pasta

This recipe takes its roots from Kasha, an Eastern European dish that is really filling and satisfying. Buckwheat is very nutritious, being packed with flavonoids and high in magnesium. Combining it with pasta and vegetables helps to lighten the porridge-like texture of pure buckwheat.

Serves 4–6

25g/1oz dried well-flavoured
  mushrooms, such as ceps
500ml/17fl oz/2¼ cups boiling
  stock or water
45ml/3 tbsp vegetable oil or
  40g/1½oz/3 tbsp butter
3–4 onions, thinly sliced
250g/9oz mushrooms, sliced
300g/11oz/1½ cups whole, coarse,
  medium or fine buckwheat
200g/7oz pasta bows
salt and ground black pepper

1 Put the dried mushrooms in a bowl, pour over half the boiling stock or water and leave to stand for 20–30 minutes, until reconstituted. Remove the mushrooms from the liquid, strain and reserve the liquid.

2 Heat the oil or butter in a frying pan, add the onions and fry for 5–10 minutes, until softened and beginning to brown. Remove the onions to a plate, then add the sliced mushrooms to the pan and fry briefly. Add the soaked mushrooms and cook for 2–3 minutes. Return the onions to the pan and set aside.

SUPERFOOD TIP
Eating buckwheat may help to reduce the risk of high cholesterol and blood pressure.

3 In a large, heavy frying pan, toast the buckwheat over a high heat for 2–3 minutes, stirring. Reduce the heat.

4 Stir the remaining boiling stock or water and the reserved mushroom soaking liquid into the buckwheat, cover the pan, and cook for about 10 minutes, until the buckwheat is just tender and the liquid has been absorbed.

5 Meanwhile, cook the pasta in a large pan of salted boiling water as directed on the packet, or until just tender, then drain.

6 When the buckwheat is cooked, toss in the onions and mushrooms, and the pasta. Season and serve hot.

Buckwheat with pasta: Energy 364kcal/1529kJ; Protein 10.3g; Carbohydrate 67g, of which sugars 4g; Fat 7.3g, of which saturates 3.6g; Cholesterol 14mg; Calcium 47mg; Fibre 2.2g; Sodium 48mg.

Pasta with roasted vegetables

This simple dish, with its fabulous array of colourful vitamin- and nutrient-rich vegetables, will spruce up any cooked pasta. Roasting the vegetables intensifies the flavours and caramelizes the natural sugars, giving a real depth to the flavour with no need to add a pasta sauce.

3 Stir the halved tomatoes and chopped garlic into the vegetable mixture, then roast for 20 minutes more, stirring once or twice. Meanwhile, cook the pasta according to the instructions on the packet.

4 Drain the pasta and tip it into a warmed bowl. Add the roasted vegetables and the remaining oil and toss well. Serve the pasta and vegetables hot, sprinkling each portion with a few herb flowers.

Serves 4–6

1 red (bell) pepper, cut into 1cm/½in squares
1 yellow or orange (bell) pepper, cut into 1cm/½in squares
1 aubergine (eggplant), diced
2 courgettes (zucchini), diced
75ml/5 tbsp extra virgin olive oil
15ml/1 tbsp chopped fresh flat leaf parsley
5ml/1 tsp dried oregano or marjoram
250g/9oz baby Italian plum tomatoes, hulled and halved lengthways
2 garlic cloves, roughly chopped
350–400g/12–14oz/3–3½ cups dried conchiglie
salt and ground black pepper
4–6 fresh marjoram or oregano flowers, to garnish

1 Preheat the oven to 190°C/375°F/ Gas 5. Rinse the prepared peppers, aubergine and courgettes in a sieve (strainer) under cold running water, drain, then transfer the vegetables to a large roasting tin (pan).

2 Pour 45ml/3 tbsp of the olive oil over the vegetables and sprinkle with the fresh and dried herbs. Add salt and pepper to taste and stir well. Roast for about 30 minutes, stirring two or three times.

COOK'S TIP
Pasta and roasted vegetables are very good served cold, so if you have any of this dish left over, cover it tightly with clear film (plastic wrap), chill in the refrigerator overnight and serve it the next day as a salad. It would also make a particularly good salad to take on a picnic.

Pasta with roasted vegetables: Energy 319Kcal/1343kJ; Protein 8.8g; Carbohydrate 49.6g, of which sugars 8g; Fat 10.8g, of which saturates 1.6g; Cholesterol 0mg; Calcium 34mg; Fibre 4g; Sodium 9mg.

Twice-cooked tempeh

Tempeh is a heart-healthy superfood due to its phytosterol and omega-3 content. Similar to tofu, but with a nuttier, more savoury flavour and firmer texture, tempeh is cooked here with a host of superfoods – garlic, onions, peppers and spices in a delicious oriental-style tomato sauce.

Serves 4

45ml/3 tbsp vegetable oil
2 onions, finely chopped
2 garlic cloves, crushed
5ml/1 tsp fennel seeds, crushed
2.5ml/½ tsp chilli flakes
5ml/1 tsp coriander seeds, crushed
5ml/1 tsp cumin seeds, crushed
1 red (bell) pepper, seeded and
   finely chopped
450g/1lb tempeh
115g/4oz Cheddar cheese, grated

For the sauce
30ml/2 tbsp tamari soy sauce
juice of ½ lemon
45ml/3 tbsp molasses or dark
   brown sugar
30ml/2 tbsp cider (apple cider)
   vinegar
15ml/1 tbsp English (hot) mustard
90ml/6 tbsp tomato purée (paste)
150ml/¼ pint/⅔ cup water
2–3 dashes Tabasco sauce (optional)
30ml/2 tbsp chopped parsley

1 Preheat the oven to 200°C/400°F/ Gas 6. Heat 30ml/2 tbsp of the oil in a large frying pan or wok, and sauté the onions, garlic and spices for 6–7 minutes, until golden and softened. Add the pepper and cook for a further 1–2 minutes, until softened.

2 Whisk all the sauce ingredients except the parsley. Add to the pan. Simmer gently for 2–3 minutes. Finally, stir in the parsley.

3 Heat the remaining oil in a large frying pan and fry the tempeh for 2–3 minutes on each side, until golden and warmed through. Transfer to a large, shallow, heatproof serving dish.

4 Pour the finished sauce over the tempeh and sprinkle evenly with the grated cheese. Bake in the oven for approximately 10 minutes, until the cheese has melted, turned golden and is bubbling.

Twice-cooked tempeh: Energy 467Kcal/1949kJ; Protein 34g; Carbohydrate 34g, of which sugars 24g; Fat 22g, of which saturates 7g; Cholesterol 28mg; Calcium 437mg; Fibre 7.5g; Sodium 1016mg.

Mixed-bean chilli with cornbread topping

The combination of beans with grains in the yeast-free cornbread ensures that you are getting complete proteins in this one-pot, slow cooker meal. Choose your favourite superfood vegetables for the chilli and you are well on your way to five portions of vegetables in one serving.

Serves 4

115g/4oz/generous ½ cup dried
  red kidney beans
115g/4oz/generous ½ cup dried
  black-eyed beans
1 bay leaf
15ml/1 tbsp vegetable oil
1 large onion, finely chopped
1 garlic clove, crushed
5ml/1 tsp ground cumin
5ml/1 tsp chilli powder
5ml/1 tsp mild paprika
2.5ml/½ tsp dried marjoram
450g/1lb mixed vegetables such
  as potatoes, carrots, aubergines
  (eggplant), parsnips and celery
1 vegetable stock cube
400g/14oz can chopped tomatoes
15ml/1 tbsp tomato purée (paste)
salt and ground black pepper

For the cornbread topping
250g/9oz/2¼ cups fine cornmeal
30ml/2 tbsp wholemeal
  (whole-wheat) flour
7.5ml/1½ tsp baking powder
1 egg, plus 1 egg yolk,
  lightly beaten
300ml/½ pint/1¼ cups milk

1 Soak the dried beans in a large bowl of cold water for at least 6 hours, or overnight.

2 Drain the beans and rinse well. Put in a pan with 600ml/1 pint/ 2½ cups of cold water and the bay leaf. Bring to the boil and boil rapidly for 10 minutes. Turn off the heat, leave to cool for a few minutes, then put in the slow cooker pot and switch to high.

3 Heat the oil in a pan, add the onion and cook for 7–8 minutes. Add the garlic, cumin, chilli powder, paprika and marjoram and cook for 1 minute. Add to the cooking pot and stir.

4 Prepare the vegetables, peeling or trimming them as necessary, then cut into 2cm/¾ in chunks.

5 Add the vegetables to the mixture, making sure that those that may discolour, such as potatoes and parsnips, are submerged. It doesn't matter if the other vegetables are not completely covered. Cover with the lid and cook for 3 hours, or until the beans are tender.

6 Add the stock cube and chopped tomatoes to the cooking pot, then stir in the tomato purée and season with salt and ground black pepper. Replace the lid and cook for a further 30 minutes, until the mixture is at boiling point.

7 To make the topping, combine the cornmeal, flour, baking powder and a pinch of salt in a bowl. Make a well in the centre and add the egg, egg yolk and milk. Mix together well.

8 Spoon the cornbread topping over the bean mixture. Cover and cook for 1 hour, or until the topping is firm and cooked.

Mixed-bean chilli: Energy 613Kcal/2595kJ; Protein 29.6g; Carbohydrate 97.4g, of which sugars 15.8g; Fat 14.5g, of which saturates 3.4g; Cholesterol 112mg; Calcium 257mg; Fibre 13.4g; Sodium 413mg.

Garlic-flavoured lentils with carrots and sage

The combination of healing sage and wholesome green lentils is very traditional, and with the addition of antioxidant-rich carrots, onions and garlic is delicious. Serve this with a dollop of bio-yogurt seasoned with crushed garlic, salt and pepper, and lemon wedges for squeezing.

Serves 4–6

175g/6oz/¾ cup green lentils, rinsed and picked over
45–60ml/3–4 tbsp fruity olive oil
1 onion, cut in half lengthways, in half again crossways, and sliced along the grain
3–4 plump garlic cloves, roughly chopped and bruised with the flat side of a knife
5ml/1 tsp coriander seeds
a handful of dried sage leaves
5–10ml/1–2 tsp sugar
4 carrots, sliced
15–30ml/1–2 tbsp tomato purée (paste)
salt and ground black pepper
1 bunch of fresh sage or flat leaf parsley, to garnish

1 Bring a pan of water to the boil and add the lentils. Lower the heat, partially cover the pan and simmer for 10 minutes. Drain and rinse well under cold running water.

2 Heat the oil in a heavy pan, stir in the onion, garlic, coriander, sage and sugar, and cook until the onion begins to colour. Toss in the carrots and cook for 2–3 minutes.

3 Add the lentils and pour in 250ml/8fl oz/1 cup water, making sure the lentils and carrots are covered. Stir in the tomato purée and cover the pan, then cook the lentils and carrots gently for about 20 minutes, until most of the liquid has been absorbed. The lentils and carrots should both be tender, but still have some bite. Season with salt and pepper to taste.

4 Garnish with the fresh sage or flat leaf parsley, and serve hot or at room temperature.

SUPERFOOD TIP
Lentils are a good source of iron, folate and magnesium.

Garlic-flavoured lentils: Energy 166kcal/696kJ; Protein 7.6g; Carbohydrate 21.1g, of which sugars 6.7g; Fat 6.2g, of which saturates 0.9g; Cholesterol 0mg; Calcium 38mg; Fibre 4g; Sodium 22mg.

Stir-fried seeds and vegetables

The multitude of seeds in this recipe will provide all of the essential fatty acids the body needs, and the colourful vegetables make it very pleasing to the eye. For a more substantial meal, try this with buckwheat noodles for some useful slow-release carbohydrate.

3 Add the watercress or spinach with the fresh herbs and toss over the heat for 1 minute.

4 Stir in the black bean sauce, soy sauce and vinegar. Stir-fry for 1–2 minutes, until combined and hot. Serve immediately.

SUPERFOOD TIPS
• Crushing the hemp seeds allows the nutrient-rich omega-3 oils to be released
• Oyster mushrooms are delicate, so it is usually better to tear them into pieces along the lines of the gills, rather than slice them with a knife.

Serves 4

30ml/2 tbsp vegetable oil
30ml/2tbsp crushed hemp seeds
30ml/2 tbsp sesame seeds
30ml/2 tbsp sunflower seeds
30ml/2 tbsp pumpkin seeds
2 garlic cloves, finely chopped
2.5cm/1in piece fresh root ginger, peeled and finely chopped
2 large carrots, cut into batons
2 large courgettes (zucchini), cut into batons
90g/3½oz/1½ cups oyster mushrooms, broken into pieces
150g/5oz watercress or spinach leaves, coarsely chopped
bunch of fresh mint or coriander (cilantro), chopped
60ml/4 tbsp black bean sauce
30ml/2 tbsp light soy sauce
15ml/1 tbsp rice vinegar

1 Heat the oil in a wok. Add the seeds. Toss over a medium heat for 1 minute, then add the garlic and ginger, and continue to stir-fry until the ginger is aromatic and the garlic is golden.

2 Add the carrot and courgette batons and mushroom pieces to the wok and stir-fry over a medium heat for a further 5 minutes, or until all the vegetables are crisp-tender and golden at the edges.

Stir-fried seeds and vegetabeles: Energy 205kcal/849kJ; Protein 6.9g; Carbohydrate 9.7g, of which sugars 7.7g; Fat 15.6g, of which saturates 2g; Cholesterol 0mg; Calcium 159mg; Fibre 3.4g; Sodium 294mg.

Thai vegetable curry with lemon grass rice

This rich, spicy recipe is jam-packed with antioxidant-rich vegetables, spices and herbs, including lemon grass. Although the ingredient list is long, it is a simple curry to make and well worth the effort. Simply change the vegetables to suit the seasons or to cater for whatever is in your refrigerator.

Serves 4

10ml/2 tsp vegetable oil
400ml/14fl oz/1⅔ cups
    coconut milk
300ml/½ pint/1¼ cups
    vegetable stock
225g/8oz new potatoes, halved
    or quartered, if large
130g/4½oz baby corn cobs
5ml/1 tsp golden caster
    (super-fine) sugar
185g/6½oz broccoli florets
1 red (bell) pepper, seeded and
    sliced lengthways
115g/4oz spinach, tough stalks
    removed and shredded
30ml/2 tbsp chopped
    fresh coriander (cilantro)
salt and black pepper

For the spice paste
1 red chilli, seeded and chopped
3 green chillies, seeded
    and chopped
1 lemon grass stalk, outer leaves
    removed and lower 5cm/
    2in finely chopped
2 shallots, chopped
finely grated rind of 1 lime
2 garlic cloves, chopped
5ml/1 tsp ground coriander
2.5ml/½ tsp ground cumin
1cm/½in fresh galangal, finely
    chopped or 2.5ml/½ tsp dried
    (optional)
30ml/2 tbsp chopped fresh
    coriander (cilantro) leaves
15ml/1 tbsp chopped fresh
    coriander roots and
    stems (optional)

For the rice
225g/8oz/generous 1 cup jasmine
    rice, rinsed
1 lemon grass stalk, outer leaves
    removed, cut into 3 pieces
6 cardamom pods, bruised

1 Make the spice paste. Place all the ingredients in a food processor or blender and blend to a coarse paste.

2 Heat the oil in a large heavy pan and fry the spice paste for 1–2 minutes, stirring constantly. Add the coconut milk and stock, and bring to the boil.

3 Reduce the heat, add the potatoes and simmer for 15 minutes. Add the baby corn and seasoning, then cook for 2 minutes. Stir in the sugar, broccoli and red pepper, and cook for 2 minutes more, until the vegetables are tender. Stir in the shredded spinach and half the fresh coriander. Cook for 2 minutes.

4 Meanwhile, pour the rinsed rice into a large pan and add the lemon grass and cardamom pods. Pour over 475ml/16fl oz/2 cups water.

5 Bring to the boil, then reduce the heat, cover, and cook for 10–15 minutes, until the water is absorbed and the rice is tender and slightly sticky. Season with salt.

6 Leave the rice to stand for 10 minutes, then fluff it up with a fork.

7 Remove the spices and serve the rice with the curry, sprinkled with the remaining fresh coriander.

Thai vegetable curry: Energy 279Kcal/1161kJ; Protein 9.8g; Carbohydrate 17.4g, of which sugars 13.3g; Fat 19.4g, of which saturates 3.6g; Cholesterol 5mg; Calcium 99mg; Fibre 3.3g; Sodium 824mg.

Mixed bean and aubergine tagine

The ingredients In this satisfying vegetarian Moroccan dish are slow-cooked, producing a rich and sumptuous sauce. Full of texture, this dish is packed with cholesterol-lowering fibre from the beans and the flavour is enhanced by the chillies and herbs. It shows you can eat well without eating meat.

Serves 4

115g/4oz/generous ½ cup dried
   red kidney beans, soaked
   overnight in cold water
   and drained
115g/4oz/generous ½ cup dried
   black-eyed beans (peas) or
   cannellini beans, soaked
   overnight in cold water
   and drained
600ml/1 pint/2½ cups water
2 bay leaves
2 celery sticks, each cut into
   4 matchsticks
60ml/4 tbsp olive oil
1 aubergine (eggplant), about
   350g/12oz, cut into chunks
1 onion, thinly sliced
3 garlic cloves, crushed
1–2 fresh red chillies, seeded
   and chopped
30ml/2 tbsp tomato purée (paste)
5ml/1 tsp paprika
2 large tomatoes,
   roughly chopped
300ml/½ pint/1¼ cups
   vegetable stock
15ml/1 tbsp each chopped fresh
   mint, parsley and coriander
   (cilantro)
ground black pepper
fresh herb sprigs, to garnish

1 Place the soaked and drained kidney beans in a large pan of unsalted boiling water. Bring back to the boil and cook the beans for 10 minutes, then drain.

2 Place the soaked and drained black-eyed or cannellini beans in a separate large pan of boiling unsalted water. Boil the beans rapidly for 10 minutes, then drain.

3 Place the water in a large tagine or casserole, and add the bay leaves, celery and beans. Cover and place in the oven at 190°C/375°FGas 5. Cook for 1–1½ hours, or until the beans are tender, then drain.

4 Heat 45ml/3 tbsp of the oil in a frying pan or cast-iron tagine base. Add the aubergine chunks and cook, stirring for 4–5 minutes until evenly browned. Remove from the heat and set aside.

5 Add the remaining oil to the frying pan or tagine base. Add the sliced onion and cook 4–5 minutes, until softened. Add the garlic and chillies and cook for a further 5 minutes.

6 Reset the oven temperature to 160°C/325°F/Gas 3. Add the tomato purée and paprika to the onion mixture and cook for 1–2 minutes. Add the tomatoes, aubergine, cooked beans and stock to the pan, then season to taste.

7 Cover the tagine base with the lid or, if using a frying pan, transfer the contents to a clay tagine or casserole. Bake in the oven for 1 hour.

8 Just before serving, add the fresh mint, parsley and coriander and lightly stir through the vegetables. Garnish with fresh herbs.

Mixed bean tagine: Energy 209Kcal/890kJ; Protein 16.6g; Carbohydrate 33.9g, of which sugars 9.4g; Fat 1.9g, of which saturates 0.5g; Cholesterol 1mg; Calcium 173mg; Fibre 12.3g; Sodium 62mg.

Pea and mint omelette

Peas and mint have long shared a plate, and this deliciously light omelette is perfect if your appetite is reduced. The eggs provide plenty of nourishment, while the peas are rich in vitamins. Serve with a green salad for a fresh and tasty lunch. For extra carbohydrate, add halved boiled baby new potatoes.

Serves 2

4 eggs
50g/2oz/½ cup frozen peas
30ml/2 tbsp chopped fresh mint
a knob (pat) of butter
salt and ground black pepper

1 Break the eggs into a large bowl and beat with a fork. Season well with salt and pepper and set aside.

2 Cook the peas in a large pan of salted boiling water for 3–4 minutes, until tender. Drain well and add to the eggs in the bowl. Stir in the chopped fresh mint and swirl with a spoon until thoroughly combined.

3 Heat the butter in a frying pan until foamy. Pour in the egg, peas and mint, and cook over a medium heat for 3–4 minutes, until the mixture is nearly set.

4 Finish cooking the omelette under a hot grill (broiler) until set and golden on top. Fold the omelette over, transfer to a warmed plate, cut it in half and serve immediately.

VARIATIONS
• Vegetable omelettes are full of goodness: try a mixture of tiny fresh or frozen cauliflower or broccoli florets, fresh peas, skinned broad (fava) beans and sliced spring onions (scallions). Cook diced red or green (bell) peppers in a little olive oil until softened.
• Cannellini beans or chickpeas go well with the vegetables, to add carbohydrate and protein.
• Add cooked small pasta shapes.

Pea and mint omelette: Energy 205kcal/851kJ; Protein 14.3g; Carbohydrate 2.9g, of which sugars 0.6g; Fat 15.6g, of which saturates 5.8g; Cholesterol 391mg; Calcium 63mg; Fibre 1.2g; Sodium 171mg.

Sardine frittata

This recipe separates the eggs which makes for a very light omelette-style dish. Bursting with flavour, this frittata is rich in brain food as it contains omega-3 oils from the sardines and choline from the eggs. Vary the taste and boost the superfood content by adding chopped peppers or tomatoes.

2 Separate the eggs. In a bowl, whisk the yolks lightly with the parsley, chives and a little salt and pepper. Beat the whites in a separate bowl with a pinch of salt until fairly stiff. Preheat the grill (broiler) to medium-high.

3 Heat the remaining olive oil in a large frying pan, add the garlic and cook over a low heat until just golden. Gently mix together the egg yolks and whites, and ladle half the mixture into the pan.

4 Cook gently until just beginning to set on the base, then lay the sardines on the frittata and sprinkle lightly with paprika. Pour over the remaining egg mixture and cook gently until the frittata has browned underneath and is beginning to set on the top.

5 Put the pan under the grill and cook until the top of the frittata turns golden. Cut into wedges and serve immediately.

Serves 4

4 fat sardines, cleaned, filleted
  and with heads removed,
  thawed if frozen
juice of 1 lemon
45ml/3 tbsp olive oil
6 large (US extra large) eggs
30ml/2 tbsp chopped fresh parsley
30ml/2 tbsp chopped fresh chives
1 garlic clove, chopped
salt, ground black pepper
  and paprika

1 Open out the sardines and sprinkle the fish with lemon juice, a little salt and paprika. Heat 15ml/1 tbsp olive oil in a frying pan and fry the sardines for about 1–2 minutes on each side to seal them. Drain on kitchen paper, trim off the tails and set aside until required.

COOK'S TIP
It is important to use a frying pan with a handle that can be used safely under the grill (broiler). If your frying pan has a wooden handle, wrap foil around it for protection.

Sardine frittata: Energy 342kcal/1422kJ; Protein 28.9g; Carbohydrate 0.2g, of which sugars 0.2g; Fat 25.3g, of which saturates 6g; Cholesterol 285mg; Calcium 137mg; Fibre 0.4g; Sodium 220mg.

Chilli-herb seared scallops

Tender, succulent scallops taste superb when marinated in a stimulating blend of fresh chilli, fragrant mint and aromatic basil. To get the best results, sear the scallops quickly in a piping-hot wok; stir-frying the pak choi retains its excellent nutrient content.

Serves 4

20–24 king scallops, cleaned
60ml/4 tbsp olive oil
finely grated rind and juice of
　1 lemon
30ml/2 tbsp finely chopped mixed
　fresh mint and basil
1 fresh red chilli, seeded and
　finely chopped
salt and ground black pepper
500g/1¼lb pak choi (bok choy)

4 Cook the scallops for 1 minute on each side, or until cooked to your liking. Pour the marinade over the scallops.

5 When the marinade has sizzled for a moment, remove the wok from the heat. Transfer the scallops and juices to a platter and keep warm. Wipe out the wok with a piece of kitchen paper.

6 Place the wok over a high heat. When all traces of moisture have evaporated, add the remaining oil. When the oil is hot, add the pak choi and stir-fry over a high heat for 2–3 minutes, until the leaves wilt.

7 Divide the greens among four warmed serving plates, then top with the reserved scallops and their juices, and serve immediately.

1 Place the scallops in a shallow, non-metallic bowl in a single layer. In a clean bowl, mix together half the oil, the lemon rind and juice, chopped herbs and chilli, and spoon over the scallops. Season well with salt and black pepper, cover and set aside.

2 Using a sharp knife, cut each pak choi lengthways into four pieces.

3 Heat a wok over a high heat. When hot, drain the scallops (reserving the marinade) and add to the wok.

Chilli-herb seared scallops: Energy 410kcal/1714kJ; Protein 44.5g; Carbohydrate 8.3g, of which sugars 2.1g; Fat 22.3g, of which saturates 3.5g; Cholesterol 82mg; Calcium 286mg; Fibre 3.2g; Sodium 494mg.

Trout with almonds

The combination of almonds and trout is very traditional and the simplicity of this dish is the key to its success. This tasty, easy-to-prepare meal is extremely good for your heart, as the cholesterol-lowering almonds complement the omega 3 from the trout.

Serves 4

4 whole trout
45–60ml/3–4 tbsp seasoned plain (all-purpose) flour
75g/3oz/6 tbsp butter
15ml/1 tbsp olive oil
50g/2oz/½ cup flaked almonds
juice of ½ lemon
lemon wedges, to serve

1 Wash the fish, dry with kitchen paper and coat them with seasoned flour, shaking off any excess.

2 Heat half the butter with the oil in a large frying pan. When the mixture begins to foam, add one or two fish. Cook over medium heat for 3–5 minutes on each side, or until golden brown and cooked through. Lift out, drain on kitchen paper and keep warm.

COOK'S TIP
Be sure to choose a trout that will fit inside your frying pan.

3 Cook the remaining fish, then wipe the pan out with kitchen paper. Add the remaining butter and, when foaming, add the almonds. Cook gently, stirring frequently, until the almonds are golden brown. Remove from the heat and add the lemon juice.

4 Sprinkle the almonds and pan juices over the trout, and serve immediately with lemon wedges for squeezing over.

VARIATION
The trout can be grilled (broiled) if preferred. Omit the flour coating. Melt half the butter and brush over both sides of the fish. Put the fish under a medium-hot grill (broiler) and cook for 5–7 minutes on each side until golden brown and cooked all the way through. Cook the almonds in butter as in step 4 above.

Trout with almonds: Energy 475kcal/1978kJ; Protein 39.2g; Carbohydrate 7.6g, of which sugars 0.8g; Fat 32.2g, of which saturates 12.4g; Cholesterol 187mg; Calcium 101mg; Fibre 1.2g; Sodium 249mg.

Salmon and rice gratin

This all-in-one supper dish is a great way of serving salmon, especially if you are a catering for a larger number. Using wild salmon ensures that you are getting the best source of omega 3 as well as the tastiest. The eggs in this dish provide an additional omega-3 boost.

Serves 6

675g/1½lb fresh wild salmon
   fillet, skinned
1 bay leaf
a few parsley stalks
1 litre/1¾ pints/4 cups water
400g/14oz/2 cups basmati rice,
   soaked and drained
30–45ml/2–3 tbsp chopped fresh
   parsley, plus extra to garnish
175g/6oz/1½ cups grated
   Cheddar cheese
3 hard-boiled eggs, chopped
sea salt and ground black pepper

For the sauce
1 litre/1¾ pints/4 cups milk
40g/1½oz/⅓ cup plain
   (all-purpose) flour
40g/1½oz/3 tbsp butter
5ml/1 tsp mild curry paste

1 Put the salmon fillet in a wide, shallow pan. Add the bay leaf and parsley stalks, with a little salt and plenty of black pepper. Pour in the water and bring to simmering point. Poach the fish for about 12 minutes until just tender.

2 Lift the salmon fillet out of the pan using a slotted spoon, then strain the cooking liquid into a large pan. Leave the fish to cool, then remove any visible bones and flake the flesh gently into bitesize pieces with a fork.

3 Add the rice to the pan of fish-poaching liquid. Bring the liquid to the boil, then lower the heat, cover tightly with a lid and simmer gently for 10 minutes without lifting the lid.

4 Remove the pan from the heat and, without lifting the lid, allow the rice to stand, undisturbed, for 5 minutes.

5 Meanwhile, make the sauce. Mix the milk, flour and butter in a pan. Bring to the boil over a low heat, whisking constantly until the sauce is smooth and thick. Stir in the curry paste with salt and pepper to taste. Simmer for 2 minutes.

6 Preheat the grill (broiler). Remove the sauce from the heat and stir in the chopped parsley and rice, with half the cheese. Fold in the flaked fish and eggs. Spoon into a shallow gratin dish and sprinkle with the remaining cheese. Cook under the grill until the topping is golden brown. Serve garnished with chopped parsley.

Salmon gratin: Energy 752Kcal/3137kJ; Protein 44.8g; Carbohydrate 66.5g, of which sugars 8.2g; Fat 33.5g, of which saturates 14.5g; Cholesterol 204mg; Calcium 492mg; Fibre 0.6g; Sodium 411mg.

Baked salmon with guava sauce

Guavas have a creamy flesh with a slight citrus tang, perfect for serving with salmon. Keep the cooking time of the guava sauce to a minimum to retain as much vitamin C as possible. Green guavas should be left in a warm place for a few days until they ripen.

Serves 4

6 ripe guavas
45ml/3 tbsp vegetable oil
1 small onion, finely chopped
120ml/4fl oz/½ cup well-flavoured
  chicken stock
10ml/2 tsp hot pepper sauce
4 salmon steaks
salt and ground black pepper
strips of red pepper to garnish

COOK'S TIP

Ripe guavas have yellow skin and succulent flesh that ranges in colour from white to deep-pink or salmon-red. Ripe fruit will keep in the fridge for a few days.

1 Cut each guava in half. Scoop the seeded soft flesh into a sieve (strainer) placed over a bowl. Press it through the sieve, discard the seeds and skin and set the pulp aside.

2 Heat 30ml/2 tbsp of the oil in a frying pan. Fry the chopped onion for about 4 minutes over a moderate heat until softened and turned translucent.

3 Stir in the guava pulp, with the chicken stock and hot pepper sauce. Cook, stirring constantly, until the sauce thickens. Keep it warm until needed.

4 Brush the salmon steaks on one side with a little of the remaining oil. Season them with salt and pepper. Heat a griddle pan until very hot and add the salmon steaks, oiled side down. Cook for 2–3 minutes, until the underside is golden, then brush the surface with oil, turn each salmon steak over and cook the other side until the fish is cooked and flakes easily.

5 Transfer each steak to a warmed plate. Serve, garnished with strips of red pepper on a pool of sauce. A fresh green salad is a good accompaniment.

Baked salmon: Energy 389Kcal/1621kJ; Protein 31.7g; Carbohydrate 8.7g, of which sugars 8.2g; Fat 25.5g, of which saturates 3.8g; Cholesterol 75mg; Calcium 55mg; Fibre 5.8g; Sodium 76mg.

Warm niçoise noodle salad with seared tuna

The meaty texture of fresh tuna steaks cooked on a griddle or a barbecue is a fabulous way to include more omega 3-rich fish in the diet. This recipe takes the traditional goodness of the niçoise salad ingredients and adds noodles to make a more filling dish.

Serves 4

2 fresh tuna steaks, each weighing about 225g/8oz
175g/6oz fine green beans, trimmed
3 eggs
350g/12oz medium Chinese dried egg noodles
225g/8oz baby plum tomatoes, halved
50g/2oz can anchovy fillets, drained and fillets separated (optional)
50g/2oz/½ cup small black olives
a handful of fresh basil leaves, torn
salt and ground black pepper

For the marinade
30ml/2 tbsp lemon juice
75ml/5 tbsp olive oil
2 garlic cloves, crushed

For the warm dressing
90ml/6 tbsp extra virgin olive oil
30ml/2 tbsp wine vinegar or lemon juice
2 garlic cloves, crushed
2.5ml/½ tsp Dijon mustard
30ml/2 tbsp capers
45ml/3 tbsp chopped herbs such as tarragon, chives, basil and chervil

1 To make the marinade, combine the lemon juice, olive oil and garlic in a glass or china dish. Add salt and pepper and mix well. Add the tuna and coat with the marinade. Cover and leave to marinate in a cool place for 1 hour.

2 Whisk all the ingredients for the dressing together in a small pan and leave to infuse. Meanwhile, blanch the green beans in boiling salted water for 4 minutes. Drain and refresh in cold water.

3 In a separate pan, cover the eggs with plenty of cold water. Bring to the boil, then boil for 10 minutes. Immediately, drain and cover with cold water to stop the cooking. When cool, shell and quarter the eggs.

4 Put the noodles and blanched beans into a bowl and pour boiling water over to cover. Leave for 5 minutes, then fork over the noodles. Heat the dressing and keep warm. Drain the noodles and beans, and toss with the dressing.

5 Heat a ridged griddle pan or heavy skillet until smoking. Drain the tuna steaks, pat dry and sear for 1–2 minutes on each side. Remove and immediately slice thinly. Add the tuna, tomatoes, anchovies and black olives to the noodles and beans, and toss well. Pile the salad into warmed serving bowls and scatter with the quartered eggs and basil. Season and eat while it is still warm.

Warm niçoise noodle salad: Energy 899Kcal/3761kJ; Protein 48g; Carbohydrate 67g, of which sugars 5g; Fat 5g, of which saturates 10g; Cholesterol 239mg; Calcium 154mg; Fibre 4.6g; Sodium 1099mg.

Smoked haddock with mustard cabbage

This simple, quick and easy-to-prepare smoked haddock recipe is really delicious. Steaming the cabbage ensures that all of its super vitamins and nutrients are retained, and gently poaching the haddock makes this a light, easily digestible dish.

2 Meanwhile, put the haddock in a large shallow pan with the milk, onion and bay leaves. Add the lemon slices and peppercorns. Bring to simmering point, cover and poach until the fish flakes easily. Depending on the thickness of the fish, this takes 8–10 minutes. Remove the pan from the heat. Preheat the grill (broiler).

3 Cut the tomatoes in half horizontally, season them with salt and pepper, and grill (broil) until lightly browned. Drain the cabbage, rinse in cold water and drain again.

4 Melt the butter in a shallow pan or wok, add the cabbage and toss over the heat for 2 minutes. Mix in the mustard and season to taste, then transfer to a warm serving dish.

Serves 4

1 Savoy or pointu cabbage
675g/1½lb undyed smoked
  haddock fillet
300ml/½ pint/1¼ cups milk
½ onion, sliced into rings
2 bay leaves
½ lemon, sliced
4 white peppercorns
4 ripe tomatoes
50g/2oz/¼ cup butter
30ml/2 tbsp wholegrain mustard
juice of 1 lemon
salt and ground black pepper
30ml/2 tbsp chopped fresh parsley,
  to garnish

1 Cut the cabbage in half, remove the central core and thick ribs, then shred the cabbage. Cook in a pan of lightly salted, boiling water, or steam over boiling water for about 10 minutes, until just tender. Leave in the pan or steamer until required.

5 Drain the haddock. Skin and cut the fish into four pieces. Place on top of the cabbage with some onion rings and grilled tomato halves. Pour on the lemon juice, then sprinkle with chopped parsley and serve.

Smoked haddock: Energy 319kcal/1340kJ; Protein 36.1g; Carbohydrate 14.2g, of which sugars 13.7g; Fat 13.1g, of which saturates 7.3g; Cholesterol 90mg; Calcium 146mg; Fibre 4.2g; Sodium 1512mg.

Fish pie with sweet potato topping

Combining sweet potatoes with normal potatoes is a great way to add another vegetable to a recipe. This tasty dish is full of contrasting flavours – the slightly spicy sweet potato making an interesting, brightly coloured topping for the mild-flavoured fish.

Serves 4

175g/6oz/scant 1 cup basmati
   rice, soaked
450ml/¾ pint/scant 2 cups
   well-flavoured stock
175g/6oz/1½ cups podded
   broad (fava) beans
675g/1½ lb haddock or cod
   fillets, skinned
about 450ml/¾ pint/scant
   2 cups milk

For the sauce
40g/1½ oz/3 tbsp butter
30–45ml/2–3 tbsp plain
   (all-purpose) flour
15ml/1 tbsp chopped fresh parsley
salt and freshly ground black
   pepper

For the topping
450g/1lb sweet potatoes, peeled
   and cut into large chunks
450g/1lb floury white potatoes,
   such as King Edwards, peeled
   and cut into large chunks
milk and butter, for mashing
10ml/2 tsp freshly chopped parsley
5ml/1 tsp freshly chopped dill

1 Preheat the oven to 190°C/375°F/ Gas 5. Drain the rice and put it in a pan. Pour in the stock, with a little salt and pepper, if needed, and bring to the boil. Cover the pan, lower the heat and simmer for 10 minutes, or until all the liquid has been absorbed.

2 Cook the broad beans in a little lightly salted water until tender. Drain thoroughly. When cool enough to handle, pop the bright green beans out of their skins.

3 To make the potato topping, boil the sweet and white potatoes separately in salted water until tender. Drain them both, then mash them with a little milk and butter. Spoon the mashed potatoes into separate bowls. Beat parsley and dill into the sweet potatoes.

4 Place the fish in a large frying pan and pour in enough of the milk (about 350ml/12fl oz/1½ cups) to just cover. Dot with 15g/½oz/1 tbsp of the butter, and season. Heat gently and simmer for 5–6 minutes, until the fish is just tender.

5 Lift out the fish and break it into large pieces. Pour the cooking liquid into a measuring jug (cup) and make up to 450ml/¾ pint/scant 2 cups with the remaining milk.

6 To make a white sauce, melt the butter in a saucepan, stir in the flour and cook for 1 minute. Gradually add the cooking liquid and milk mixture, stirring, until a fairly thin white sauce is formed. Stir in the parsley and season to taste.

7 Spread out the cooked rice on the bottom of a large oval gratin dish. Add the broad beans and fish, and pour over the white sauce. Spoon the mashed potatoes over the top, to make an attractive pattern. Dot with a little extra butter and bake for 15 minutes until lightly browned.

Fish pie: Energy 604Kcal/2545kJ; Protein 41.6g; Carbohydrate 88g, of which sugars 8.6g; Fat 10.7g, of which saturates 5.7g; Cholesterol 99mg; Calcium 94mg; Fibre 6.9g; Sodium 223mg.

Chicken with chickpeas and almonds

The chicken and chickpeas in this tasty Moroccan-style recipe are both excellent low-fat protein sources, while the heart-healthy almonds are low in saturated fats. This dish goes well with vegetable cous cous or with warmed wholemeal pitta bread.

Serves 4

75g/3oz/½ cup blanched almonds
75g/3oz/½ cup chickpeas, soaked
  overnight and drained
4 chicken breast portions, skinned
30ml/2 tbsp olive oil
2.5ml/½ tsp saffron threads
2 Spanish (Bermuda) onions, sliced
900ml/1½ pints/3¾ cups chicken
  stock
1 small cinnamon stick
60ml/4 tbsp chopped fresh
  flat leaf parsley, plus extra
  to garnish
lemon juice, to taste
salt and freshly ground
  black pepper

1 Place the blanched almonds and the chickpeas in a large flameproof casserole of water and bring to the boil. Boil for 10 minutes, then reduce the heat. Simmer for 1–1½ hours, until the chickpeas are soft. Drain and set aside.

COOK'S TIP
To save time, use a small can of chickpeas instead of the dried variety. This avoids having to soak the chickpeas overnight or simmer them until soft. Simply boil with the blanched almonds for 10 minutes and go to step 2.

2 Place the skinned chicken pieces in the casserole, together with the olive oil, half of the saffron, and salt and plenty of black pepper. Heat gently, stirring constantly until warmed through.

3 Add the onions and stock, bring to the boil, then add the reserved cooked almonds, chickpeas and cinnamon stick. Cover with a tightly fitting lid and cook very gently for 45–60 minutes, until the chicken is completely tender.

4 Transfer the chicken breasts to a serving plate and keep warm. Bring the sauce to the boil and cook over a high heat until it is well reduced, stirring frequently.

5 Add the chopped parsley and remaining saffron to the casserole and cook for a further 2–3 minutes. Sharpen the sauce with a little lemon juice, then pour the sauce over the chicken and serve, garnished with extra fresh parsley.

Chicken with chickpeas: Energy 431kcal/1803kJ; Protein 44.4g; Carbohydrate 11g, of which sugars 1.6g; Fat 23.6g, of which saturates 7.9g; Cholesterol 132mg; Calcium 110mg; Fibre 4g; Sodium 180mg.

Penne with chicken, broccoli and cheese

The delicious combination of broccoli, garlic and Gorgonzola is very moreish, and goes especially well with the chicken. The broccoli is cooked very quickly, which locks in vital nutrients, including vitamin C, which helps the body to absorb the iron and calcium in the chicken and cheese.

Serves 4

115g/4oz/scant 1 cup broccoli
   florets, divided into tiny sprigs
30ml/2 tbsp olive oil
2 skinless chicken breast fillets,
   cut into thin strips
2 garlic cloves, crushed
400g/14oz/3½ cups dried penne
120ml/4fl oz/½ cup dry white wine
200ml/7fl oz/scant 1 cup panna da
   cucina or double (heavy) cream
90g/3½oz Gorgonzola cheese,
   rind removed and diced small
salt and ground black pepper
freshly grated Parmesan cheese,
   to serve

1 Plunge the broccoli into a pan of boiling salted water. Bring back to the boil and cook for 2 minutes.

2 Drain in a colander and refresh under cold running water. Shake well to remove the surplus water and set aside to drain completely.

3 Heat the olive oil in a large skillet or pan, add the chicken and garlic with salt and pepper to taste, and stir well. Fry over a medium heat for 3 minutes, or until the chicken becomes white.

4 Start cooking the pasta according to the instructions on the packet.

5 Pour the wine and cream over the chicken mixture in the pan, stir to mix, then simmer, stirring occasionally, for about 5 minutes, until the sauce has reduced and thickened.

6 Add the broccoli, then increase the heat and toss gently to warm it through and mix it with the chicken. Season according to taste.

7 Drain the pasta and pour it into the sauce. Add the Gorgonzola and toss well. Top with grated Parmesan cheese to serve.

VARIATION
Try using leeks instead of broccoli if you prefer. Simply fry them with the chicken.

Penne with chicken: Energy 951Kcal/3982kJ; Protein 47.8g; Carbohydrate 80.2g, of which sugars 8.6g; Fat 48.8g, of which saturates 28.5g; Cholesterol 165mg; Calcium 324mg; Fibre 10.2g; Sodium 433mg.

Turkey and broccoli lasagne

The low-fat, protein-rich turkey in this easy meal-in-one pasta bake is healthier than the more traditional minced beef variant. Adding broccoli adds to its nutritional credentials and the intense flavour of Parmesan means that a little cheese goes a long way.

3 To make the sauce, melt the butter in a pan, stir in the flour and cook for 1 minute, still stirring. Remove from the heat and gradually stir in the milk. Return to the heat and gently bring the sauce to the boil, stirring constantly. Simmer for 1 minute, then add 50g/2oz/⅔ cup of the Parmesan together with plenty of salt and pepper.

4 Spoon a layer of the turkey mixture into a large, deep baking dish. Add a layer of broccoli and cover with sheets of lasagne. Coat with cheese sauce. Repeat these layers, finishing with a layer of cheese sauce on top. Sprinkle with the remaining Parmesan and bake for 35–40 minutes.

Serves 4

30ml/2 tbsp light olive oil
1 onion, chopped
2 garlic cloves, chopped
450g/1lb cooked turkey meat,
 finely diced
225g/8oz/1 cup mascarpone
 cheese
30ml/2 tbsp chopped
 fresh tarragon
300g/11oz broccoli, broken
 into florets
115g/4oz no pre-cook
 lasagne verde
salt and ground black pepper

For the sauce

50g/2oz/¼ cup butter
30ml/2 tbsp flour
600ml/1 pint/2½ cups milk
75g/3oz/1 cup freshly grated
 Parmesan cheese

1 Preheat the oven to 180°C/350°F/ Gas 4. Heat the oil in a heavy pan and cook the onion and garlic until softened but not coloured. Remove the pan from the heat and stir in the turkey, mascarpone and tarragon, with seasoning to taste.

2 Blanch the broccoli in a large pan of salted boiling water for 1 minute, then drain and rinse thoroughly under cold water to prevent the broccoli from overcooking. Drain well and set aside.

> **COOK'S TIP**
> This is a delicious way of using up any cooked turkey that is left over after Christmas or Thanksgiving celebrations. It is also good made with half ham and half turkey.

Turkey lasagne: Energy 732Kcal/3072kJ; Protein 61.6g; Carbohydrate 43g, of which sugars 13.1g; Fat 36.2g, of which saturates 19.4g; Cholesterol 138mg; Calcium 539mg; Fibre 3.6g; Sodium 475mg.

Beef casserole with baby onions and red wine

The fragrant, rich aromas that will fill the kitchen from this dish will make your mouth water. The slow cooking of the beef ensures that much of the fat melts away, leaving tender meat and a rich sauce, but it will not destroy the cardioprotective resveratrol in the red wine.

Serves 4

75ml/5 tbsp olive oil
1kg/2¼lb stewing or braising
  steak, cut into large cubes
3 garlic cloves, chopped
5ml/1 tsp ground cumin
5cm/2in piece of cinnamon stick
175ml/6fl oz/¾ cup red wine
30ml/2 tbsp red wine vinegar
small fresh rosemary sprig
2 bay leaves, crumbled
30ml/2 tbsp tomato purée (paste),
  diluted in 1 litre/1¾ pints/
  4 cups hot water
675g/1½lb small pickling onions,
  peeled and left whole
15ml/1 tbsp demerara (raw) sugar
salt and ground black pepper

COOK'S TIP
This dish can also be cooked in the oven. Use a flameproof casserole. Having browned the meat and added the remaining ingredients, with the exception of the onions and sugar, put the covered casserole in an oven preheated to 160°C/325°F/Gas 3. Bake for about 2 hours, or until the meat is tender. Add the onions and sugar as in steps 4 and 5 above. Return the casserole to the oven. Cook for 1 hour.

1 Heat the olive oil in a large heavy pan and brown the meat cubes, in batches if necessary, until pale golden brown all over.

2 Stir in the garlic and cumin. Add the cinnamon stick and cook for a few seconds, then pour the wine and vinegar slowly over the mixture. Let the liquid bubble and evaporate for 3–4 minutes.

3 Add the rosemary and bay leaves, with the diluted tomato purée. Stir well, season with salt and pepper, then cover and simmer gently for about 1½ hours, or until the meat is tender.

4 Dot the onions over the meat mixture and shake the pan to distribute them evenly.

5 Sprinkle the demerara sugar over the onions, cover the pan and cook gently for 30 minutes, until the onions are soft but have not begun to disintegrate. If necessary, add a little hot water at this stage.

6 Do not stir once the onions have been added, but gently shake the pan instead to coat them in the sauce. Serve immediately.

Beef casserole: Energy 672Kcal/2,798kJ; Protein 59.2g; Carbohydrate 18.4g, of which sugars 14.5g; Fat 37.4g, of which saturates 11.5g; Cholesterol 145mg; Calcium 62mg; Fibre 2.6g; Sodium 186mg.

Chilli con carne

Using lean braising steak and cutting off any visible fat keeps the saturated fat content down. Adding beans is great way of making expensive meat go further, and will make the recipe more nutritious. Serve with rice or tortillas to complete this hearty meal.

Serves 8

1.2kg/2½lb lean braising steak
30ml/2 tbsp sunflower or
   rapeseed oil
1 large onion, chopped
2 garlic cloves, finely chopped
15ml/1 tbsp plain (all-purpose) flour
300ml/½ pint/1¼ cups red wine
300ml/½ pint/1¼ cups beef stock
30ml/2 tbsp tomato purée (paste)
fresh coriander (cilantro) leaves,
   to garnish
salt and ground black pepper

For the beans
30ml/2 tbsp olive oil
1 onion, chopped
1 red chilli, seeded and chopped
2 x 400g/14oz cans red kidney
   beans, drained and rinsed
400g/14oz can chopped tomatoes

For the topping
6 tomatoes, peeled and chopped
1 green chilli, seeded and chopped
30ml/2 tbsp snipped fresh chives
30ml/2 tbsp chopped fresh
   coriander (cilantro)
150ml/¼ pint/⅔ cup sour cream

1 Cut the meat into thick strips and then into small cubes. Heat the oil in a large, flameproof casserole. Add the chopped onion and garlic, and cook until softened but not coloured. Season the flour then place it on a plate, then toss the meat in batches.

2 Use a draining spoon to remove the onion from the pan, then add a batch of floured beef and cook over a high heat until browned on all sides. Remove from the pan and set aside, then flour and brown another batch.

3 When the last batch of meat is browned, return the first batches with the onion to the pan. Stir in the wine, stock and tomato purée. Bring to the boil, reduce the heat and simmer for 45 minutes, or until the beef is tender.

4 Meanwhile, for the beans, heat the olive oil in a frying pan and cook the onion and chilli until softened. Add the kidney beans and tomatoes, and simmer gently for 20–25 minutes, or until thickened and reduced.

5 Mix the tomatoes, chilli, chives and coriander for the topping. Ladle the meat mixture on to warmed plates. Add a layer of bean mixture and tomato topping. Add a dollop of sour cream and garnish with coriander.

Chilli con carne: Energy 469Kcal/1963kJ; Protein 42g; Carbohydrate 28.3g, of which sugars 11.2g; Fat 18.8g, of which saturates 6.8g; Cholesterol 106mg; Calcium 127mg; Fibre 8.1g; Sodium 523mg.

Beef stew with oysters

At first glance, this dish may not seem too healthy, but oysters are a good source of omega-3 oils and grass-fed beef contains conjugated linoleic acid, both of which promote heart health. Serve with a sweet potato mash and mounds of green vegetables to ensure a good balance of nutrients.

Serves 4

1kg/2¼lb rump (round) steak
6 thin rashers (strips) streaky
   (fatty) bacon
12 oysters
50g/2oz/½ cup plain (all-purpose)
   flour
generous pinch of cayenne pepper
olive oil, for greasing
3 shallots, finely chopped
300ml/½ pint/1¼ cups beef stock
salt and freshly ground black
   pepper

1 Preheat the oven to 180°C/350°F/ Gas 4. You need thin strips of beef for this recipe, so place the steaks one at a time between sheets of clear film (plastic wrap) and beat them with a rolling pin until they are thin and flattened. Slice the meat into 24 thin strips, wide enough to roll around an oyster.

2 Stretch the bacon rashers lengthways by placing them on a chopping board and, holding one end down with your thumb, pulling them out using the thick side of a sharp knife. Cut each rasher into four pieces.

3 Remove the oysters from their shells, retaining the liquid from inside the shells in a separate container. Set aside.

4 Cut each oyster in half lengthways and roll each piece in a strip of bacon, ensuring that the bacon goes around at least once and preferably covers the oyster at each end. Then, roll in a strip of beef so no oyster is visible.

5 Season the flour with the cayenne pepper and salt and black pepper, then roll the meat in it.

6 Lightly grease a large flameproof casserole with olive oil. Sprinkle the shallots evenly over the base. Place the floured meat rolls on top, keeping them well spaced out.

7 Slowly pour over the beef stock, bring to the boil, then cover and cook in the oven for 1½–2 hours. The flour from around the meat will have thickened the stew sauce, producing a rich gravy.

Beef stew with oysters: Energy 528kcal/2208kJ; Protein 61.4g; Carbohydrate 12.7g, of which sugars 2.5g; Fat 24.4g, of which saturates 10.1g; Cholesterol 182mg; Calcium 52mg; Fibre 0.6g; Sodium 634mg.

Lamb and carrot casserole with barley

The sweet carrots in this recipe complement the lamb well, and their high carotenoid content is retained even after two hours of cooking. The cholesterol-lowering pot barley adds flavour and texture as well as helping to thicken the sauce.

2 Slice the onions and add to the pan. Fry gently for 5 minutes. Add the carrots and celery and cook for 3–4 minutes. Transfer to a casserole.

3 Sprinkle the pot barley over the vegetables in the casserole, then arrange the lamb pieces on top.

4 Lightly season with salt and ground black pepper, then sprinkle with the herbs. Pour the stock over the meat, so that all of the meat is covered.

5 Cover the casserole with the lid and cook in the oven for about 2 hours, or until the meat, vegetables and barley are tender.

6 Taste and adjust the seasoning before serving with spring cabbage and baked potatoes.

Serves 6

675g/1½lb boneless lamb
15ml/1 tbsp vegetable oil
2 onions
675g/1½lb carrots, thickly sliced
4–6 celery sticks, sliced
45ml/3 tbsp pot barley, rinsed
600ml/1 pint/2½ cups near-boiling
   lamb or vegetable stock
5ml/1 tsp fresh thyme leaves or
   pinch of dried mixed herbs
salt and ground black pepper
spring cabbage and baked
   potatoes, to serve

1 Preheat the oven to 160°C/325°F/ Gas 3. Trim the lamb. Cut the meat into 3cm/1¼in pieces. Heat the oil in a frying pan, add the lamb and fry until browned. Remove and set aside.

Lamb and carrot casserole: Energy 310kcal/1295kJ; Protein 24.2g; Carbohydrate 20.6g, of which sugars 12.2g; Fat 15.1g, of which saturates 6.2g; Cholesterol 86mg; Calcium 64mg; Fibre 3.9g; Sodium 139mg.

Moroccan lamb with honey and prunes

Even though this dish is sweet, it uses honey and prunes, which means it retains a good glycemic index. Slow roasting the lamb ensures that much of the excess fat is cooked off. A delicious accompaniment to this lamb dish would be a warm lentil salad with red onions and garlic.

Serves 6

130g/4½oz/generous ½ cup
  pitted prunes
350ml/12fl oz/1½ cups hot tea
1kg/2¼lb stewing or braising
  lamb such as shoulder, cut into
  chunky portions
1 onion, chopped
75–90ml/5–6 tbsp chopped
  fresh parsley
2.5ml/½ tsp ground ginger
2.5ml/½ tsp curry powder or
  ras el hanout
pinch of freshly grated nutmeg
10ml/2 tsp ground cinnamon
1.5ml/¼ tsp saffron threads
30ml/2 tbsp hot water
75–120ml/5–9 tbsp honey, to taste
250ml/8fl oz/1 cup beef or lamb
  stock
115g/4oz/1 cup blanched almonds,
  toasted
30ml/2 tbsp chopped fresh
  coriander (cilantro) leaves
3 hard-boiled eggs, cut into
  wedges
salt and ground black pepper

1 Preheat the oven to 180°C/350°F/ Gas 4. Put the prunes in a bowl, pour over the tea and cover. Leave to soak.

2 Meanwhile, put the lamb, chopped onion, parsley, ginger, curry powder or ras el hanout, nutmeg, cinnamon, salt and black pepper in a roasting pan. Cover and cook for about 2 hours.

3 Drain off excess fat from the lamb. Drain the prunes; add their liquid to the lamb. Combine the saffron and hot water and add to the pan with the honey and stock. Bake for 30 minutes, turning the lamb occasionally.

4 Add the prunes to the pan and stir gently to mix. Serve topped with the wedges of hard-boiled egg and sprinkled with the toasted almonds, a little curry powder or ras el hanout, and chopped coriander.

Moroccan lamb: Energy 490Kcal/2051kJ; Protein 43.6g; Carbohydrate 23.8g, of which sugars 23.4g; Fat 25.2g, of which saturates 10.3g; Cholesterol 279mg; Calcium 41mg; Fibre 1.4g; Sodium 197mg.

Pan-fried calf's liver with crisp onions

Calf's liver melts in the mouth and is a truly delicious way of eating offal. Its iron content is second to none, and serving it with any salad which includes vitamin-C-rich tomatoes will ensure that you absorb all of its goodness. Avoid cooking the liver for too long as this may cause it to toughen.

Serves 4

30ml/2 tbsp olive oil
4 onions, finely sliced
5ml/1 tsp caster (superfine) sugar
4 slices calf's liver, each weighing about 115g/4oz
30ml/2 tbsp plain (all-purpose) flour
30ml/2 tbsp olive oil
salt and ground black pepper
parsley, to garnish
sautéed potatoes, to serve

1 Heat the oil in a large, heavy pan with a tight-fitting lid. Add the onions and mix well to coat with the oil. Cover the pan and cook gently for 10 minutes, stirring occasionally.

2 Stir in the sugar and cover the pan. Cook the onions for a further 10 minutes, or until they are soft and golden.

3 Increase the heat, remove the lid and stir the onions over a high heat until they are deep gold and crisp. Use a draining spoon to remove the onions from the pan, draining off the fat.

4 Meanwhile, rinse the calf's liver slices in cold water and pat them dry on kitchen paper. Season the flour, put it on a plate and turn the slices of liver in it until they are lightly coated in flour.

5 Heat the oil in a large frying pan, add the liver and cook for about 2 minutes on each side, or until lightly browned and just firm. Arrange the cooked liver slices on warmed plates, with the crisp onions. Garnish with parsley, and serve with sautéed or mashed potatoes.

Pan-fried calf's liver: Energy 315Kcal/1310kJ; Protein 22.7g; Carbohydrate 11.8g, of which sugars 4.4g; Fat 19.9g, of which saturates 8.5g; Cholesterol 452mg; Calcium 39mg; Fibre 1.3g; Sodium 160mg.

Spicy Mexican tacos

This recipe uses textured vegetable protein, or TVP, instead of minced beef. TVP is a soya bean product that is low in fat and high in protein isoflavones, which are useful for reducing cholesterol. Chillies, tomatoes and peppers add to the superfood count.

Makes 8

5ml/1 tsp yeast extract
200ml/8floz hot water
5ml/1 tsp soy sauce
85g/3oz unflavoured textured
   vegetable protein (TVP)
1 onion, chopped
1 red (bell) pepper, finely chopped
1 garlic clove, crushed
10ml/2 tsp chilli powder
1 x 400g/14oz can chopped
   tomatoes
8 corn taco shells
shredded lettuce, chopped fresh
   tomatoes and grated cheese,
   to serve

1 Dissolve the yeast extract in the hot water and add the soy sauce and the TVP. Mix well and leave the TVP to rehydrate.

2 Fry the chopped onion, pepper and garlic in a non-stick pan until the ingredients are softened and then add the chilli powder.

3 Add the TVP mix and the chopped tomatoes and stir well, simmering for approximately 15 minutes.

4 Prepare the lettuce, tomato and grated cheese accompaniments.

5 When the tomato and TVP mixture is cooked, fill each of the taco shells with a few tablespoonfuls of the spicy sauce. Serve the tacos topped with shredded lettuce, fresh chopped tomatoes and grated cheese.

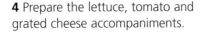

Spicy Mexican tacos: Energy 108Kcal/376kJ; Protein 4g; Carbohydrate 13g, of which sugars 4g; Fat 1g, of which saturates 2g; Cholesterol 0mg; Calcium 15mg; Fibre 1.6g; Sodium 113mg.

DESSERTS, CAKES AND DRINKS

Being conscious of your nutritional intake does not mean that you have to exclude desserts from your diet. There are a wealth of tempting sweets that can be enjoyed that provide a great opportunity to include vitamin-packed fruit in your daily menu. All fruit is good for you, whether fresh, frozen, dried or canned (ideally in natural juice), so go ahead and tuck into fruit salads, fruit puddings, frozen yogurts, sorbets and granitas.

Ginger and kiwi sorbet

Freshly grated root ginger gives a lively, aromatic flavour to sorbets and ice creams. In this recipe, stomach-soothing ginger is combined with kiwi fruit to make a vitamin C-rich sorbet. This is certainly a light, refreshing end to a meal, and especially good after a rich main course.

Serves 6

55g/2oz fresh root ginger
115g/4oz/½ cup caster
  (superfine) sugar
300ml/½ pint/1¼ cups water
5 kiwi fruit
fresh mint sprigs or chopped
kiwi fruit, to decorate

COOK'S TIP
If you keep a ginger root in the freezer, all you have to do when you need some is to snap off the required amount. Frozen ginger is also easier to grate.

1 Peel the ginger and grate it finely. Place the sugar and water in a pan and heat gently until the sugar has completely dissolved. Add the ginger and cook for 1 minute, then leave to cool. Strain the syrup into a bowl and chill until very cold.

2 Peel the kiwi fruit and blend until smooth. Add the purée to the chilled syrup and mix well.

3 By hand: Pour the mixture into a container and freeze for 3–4 hours, beating twice as it thickens. Return to the freezer until ready to serve.

Using an ice cream maker: Churn the mixture until it thickens. Transfer to a plastic tub or similar freezerproof container and freeze until ready to serve.

4 Spoon into glasses, decorate with mint sprigs or chopped kiwi fruit, and serve.

Ginger and kiwi sorbet: Energy 100Kcal/426kJ; Protein 0.7g; Carbohydrate 25.3g, of which sugars 25.2g; Fat 0.3g, of which saturates 0g; Cholesterol 0mg; Calcium 23mg; Fibre 1g; Sodium 3mg.

Strawberry snow

Strawberries have a delicate, fragrant taste and this dessert is best eaten soon after it is made. Only half the strawberries are cooked, retaining the vitamin C in the raw crushed strawberries. You can substitute the strawberries with any of your favourite superfruits such as blueberries or raspberries.

Serves 4

120ml/4fl oz/½ cup water
15ml/1 tbsp powdered gelatine
300g/11oz/2¾ cups strawberries, crushed lightly
250ml/8fl oz/1 cup double (heavy) cream
4 egg whites
90g/3½oz/½ cup caster (superfine) sugar
halved strawberries, to decorate

1 Put the water in a small bowl and sprinkle in the gelatine. Stand the bowl over a pan of hot water and heat gently until dissolved. Remove the bowl from the pan and leave to cool slightly.

2 Put half the crushed strawberries in a pan and bring to the boil. Remove from the heat, then stir in the dissolved gelatine. Chill in the refrigerator for about 2 hours until syrupy.

3 Pour the cream into a bowl and whisk until it holds its shape. Whisk the egg whites until stiff, gradually adding the sugar as they rise. Fold the egg whites into the cooled strawberry mixture, then fold in the remaining crushed strawberries, followed by the whipped cream.

4 Turn the mixture into individual serving dishes, decorate with halved strawberries, and serve immediately or chill until required.

COOK'S TIP
Strawberry Snow freezes well and can then be served as an iced strawberry parfait. All you have to do to make this is spoon the mixture into a loaf tin (pan) lined with clear film (plastic wrap), and freeze for a couple of hours, until it is firm.

Strawberry snow: Energy 443kcal/1841kJ; Protein 7.8g; Carbohydrate 29.1g, of which sugars 29.1g; Fat 33.7g, of which saturates 20.9g; Cholesterol 86mg; Calcium 56mg; Fibre 0.8g; Sodium 81mg.

Rhubarb fool

Here is a quick and simple dessert that makes the most of fibre-rich rhubarb. Although this recipe traditionally uses cream, you can substitute this with a low-fat bio-yogurt and use a low-fat custard to help to keep the fat content and calorific value to minimum.

2 Pass the rhubarb through a fine sieve (strainer) so you have a thick purée.

3 Use equal parts of the purée, the whipped double cream and thick custard. Combine the purée and custard first then fold in the cream. Chill in the refrigerator before serving. Serve with heather honey.

Serves 4

450g/1lb rhubarb, trimmed
75g/3oz/scant ½ cup soft light
    brown sugar
whipped double (heavy) cream
    and ready-made thick custard
heather honey, to serve

COOK'S TIP
Make extra quantities of fruit purée and freeze to save time the next time you make this dessert.

1 Cut the rhubarb into pieces and wash thoroughly. Stew over a low heat with just the water clinging to it and the sugar. This takes about 10 minutes. Set aside to cool.

VARIATIONS
You can use another stewed fruit if you like for this dessert – try blackberries, apples, prunes or peaches. For something a little more exotic, you could try using mangoes.

Rhubarb fool: Energy 439kcal/1828kJ; Protein 4.6g; Carbohydrate 34.1g, of which sugars 31.8g; Fat 31.7g, of which saturates 18.9g; Cholesterol 80mg; Calcium 233mg; Fibre 1.6g; Sodium 74mg.

Raspberry fromage frais and amaretti scrunch

This pudding looks stunning but is actually very simple to make. The raspberries are not cooked in this recipe, so all of the vitamin C is retained. Honey is used as a sweetener, and along with the natural fruit sugars will give this dessert a low glycaemic index.

Serves 4–6

250g/9oz/1½ cups frozen or
　fresh raspberries
500g/1¼lb/2½ cups fromage
　frais or thick natural (plain)
　bio-yogurt
30ml/2 tbsp clear honey
finely grated rind of 1 small
　lemon
75g/3oz/1½ cups amaretti, broken
　into pieces
crystallized rose petals, for
　decoration (optional)

1 If using frozen raspberries, allow them to partly defrost. If using fresh ones, partly freeze them.

2 Place the fromage frais or yogurt in a large bowl and stir in the honey and lemon rind. Add the raspberries and fold in gently, being careful not to over-mix. Chill for 1 hour.

3 Stir in the amaretti just before serving. Decorate with crystallized rose petals, if you wish.

COOK'S TIP
Gently wash the raspberries immediately before use, otherwise they will turn soggy.

VARIATION
Instead of the raspberries, try using fresh strawberries or a mix of your favourite berries.

Raspberry fromage frais: Energy 183Kcal/771kJ; Protein 5.7g; Carbohydrate 27.2g, of which sugars 21.3g; Fat 6.4g, of which saturates 3.7g; Cholesterol 17mg; Calcium 99mg; Fibre 1.2g; Sodium 72mg.

Summer berry frozen yogurt

This dessert is a fabulous, healthier and lower-fat alternative to ice cream. Any combination of sweet, juicy summer fruits can be used, and they will all contribute a wonderful array of antioxidants and vitamin C, which also helps the body to absorb the calcium from the yogurt.

Serves 6

350g/12oz/3 cups frozen summer fruits, plus whole fresh or frozen berries, to decorate
200g/7oz/scant 1 cup low-fat bio-yogurt
25g/1oz icing (confectioners') sugar

COOK'S TIP
To make a more creamy frozen yogurt, use Greek (US strained plain) yogurt. This will still be healthy, just slightly higher in fat.

1 Place all the ingredients into a food processor and process until the mixture is well combined but still quite chunky in texture. Spoon the mixture into six 150ml/¼ pint/⅔ cup ramekin dishes.

2 Cover each dish with clear film (plastic wrap) and place in the freezer for about 2 hours, or until firm.

3 To turn out the frozen yogurts, dip the ramekin dishes briefly in hot water, taking care not to allow water to get on to the dessert itself. Invert the ramekins on to small serving plates. Tap the base of the dishes and the yogurts should come out.

4 Serve the frozen yogurt immediately, decorated with fresh or frozen berries of your choice, such as blueberries, blackberries or raspberries.

Summer berry frozen yogurt: Energy 51Kcal/215kJ; Protein 2.2g; Carbohydrate 10.4g, of which sugars 10.4g; Fat 0.4g, of which saturates 0.2g; Cholesterol 0mg; Calcium 75mg; Fibre 0.7g; Sodium 32mg.

Watermelon granita

The pastel pink flakes of ice, subtly blended with the citrus freshness of lime and the delicate flavour of watermelon, make this refreshing granita a delight for the eyes as well as the tastebuds. The watermelon is rich in the antioxidant lycopene, so this is a treat for the body, too.

Serves 6

150g/5oz/⅔ cup caster (superfine) sugar
150ml/¼ pint/¾ cup water
1 whole watermelon, about 1.75kg/4–4½lb
finely grated rind and juice of 2 limes, plus lime wedges, to serve

1 Bring the sugar and water to the boil in a pan, stirring until the sugar has dissolved. Pour into a bowl. Cool, then chill. Cut the watermelon into quarters.

2 Discard most of the seeds, scoop the flesh into a food processor and process briefly until smooth. Alternatively, use a blender, and process the watermelon quarters in small batches.

3 Strain the purée into a large plastic container. Discard the seeds. Pour in the chilled syrup, lime rind and juice and mix well.

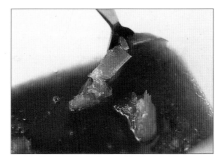

4 Cover and freeze for 2 hours, until the mixture around the sides of the container is mushy. Mash the ice finely with a fork and return the granita to the freezer.

5 Freeze for 2 hours more, mashing the mixture every 30 minutes, until the granita turns slushy. Scoop it into dishes and serve with lime wedges.

VARIATION
For an indulgent cocktail-style granita, dip the rim of each glass serving dish in a little water or beaten egg white, then dip it into sugar. Spoon in the granita, pour in a little tequila or white rum and decorate with lime wedges.

Watermelon granita: Energy 153Kcal/653kJ; Protein 1g; Carbohydrate 38g, of which sugars 38g; Fat 1g, of which saturates 0g; Cholesterol 0mg; Calcium 20mg; Fibre 0.3g; Sodium 5mg.

Peach and cardamom yogurt ice

Low-fat frozen desserts that rely on natural fruit sugar for their sweetness are perfect for diabetics. Cardamom contains volatile oils that freshen the breath, and make this dessert particularly refreshing and cleansing. Mangoes or strawberries can also be used in place of the peaches.

Serves 4

8 cardamom pods
6 peaches, total weight about 500g/1¼lb, halved and stoned (pitted)
30ml/2 tbsp water
200ml/7fl oz/scant 1 cup natural (plain) bio-yogurt

COOK'S TIP
Use natural (plain) bio-yogurt for its extra mild taste. Greek (US strained plain) yogurt or ordinary natural yogurt are both much sharper, and tend to overwhelm the delicate taste of peach.

1 Put the cardamom pods on a board and crush them with the base of a ramekin, or use a mortar and pestle.

2 Chop the peaches and put them in a pan. Add the crushed cardamom pods, with their black seeds, and the measured water. Cover and simmer gently for about 10 minutes, or until the fruit is tender. Remove the pan from the heat and leave to cool.

3 Pour the peach mixture into a food processor or blender, process until smooth, then press through a sieve (strainer) placed over a bowl.

4 Add the yogurt to the purée and mix. Pour into a freezerproof tub and freeze for about 6 hours, beating once or twice with a whisk or in a food processor. To serve, scoop the ice cream on to a platter or into bowls.

Peach and cardamom yogurt ice: Energy 69kcal/296kJ; Protein 3.8g; Carbohydrate 13.3g, of which sugars 13.3g; Fat 0.6g, of which saturates 0.3g; Cholesterol 1mg; Calcium 104mg; Fibre 1.9g; Sodium 43mg.

Date and tofu ice

Low in saturated fat and high in soya protein, this unusual dairy-free ice cream is truly heart healthy. While it also contains no added sugar, the dates and cinnamon ensure there is no compromise on flavour, and make a delicious dessert.

Serves 4

250g/9oz/1½ cups stoned
   (pitted) dates
600ml/1 pint/2½ cups apple juice
5ml/1 tsp ground cinnamon
285g/10oz pack chilled tofu,
   drained and cubed
150ml/¼ pint/⅔ cup unsweetened
   soya milk

1 Put the dates in a pan. Pour in 300ml/½ pint/1¼ cups of the apple juice and leave to soak for 2 hours. Simmer for 10 minutes, then leave to cool. Using a slotted spoon, lift out one-quarter of the dates, chop roughly and set aside.

2 Purée the remaining dates in a food processor or blender. Add the cinnamon and process with enough of the remaining apple juice to make a smooth paste.

3 Add the cubes of tofu to the food processor, a few at a time, processing after each addition. Finally, add the remaining apple juice and the soya milk and mix well to combine.

VARIATIONS
Make this ice cream with any soft dried fruits, such as figs, apricots or peaches, or use a mix of your favourite fruits.

4 Churn the mixture in an ice cream maker until very thick, but not thick enough to scoop. Scrape into a plastic tub.

5 Stir in most of the chopped dates, retaining a few pieces for garnishing, and freeze for 2–3 hours, until firm.

6 Scoop the ice cream into dessert glasses and decorate with the remaining chopped dates.

SUPERFOOD TIP
Remember that dried fruits are naturally high in sugar and can cause fluctuations in blood sugar levels. This tofu and date ice does not have added sugar, and it can be served with fresh fruit or have fresh fruit mixed in at the last minute. Try fresh strawberries, raspberries or cherries to bulk out the ice and boost its vitamin and fibre content.

Date and tofu ice: Energy 290kcal/1232kJ; Protein 9.1g; Carbohydrate 58.2g, of which sugars 57.9g; Fat 3.9g, of which saturates 0.5g; Cholesterol 0mg; Calcium 407mg; Fibre 2.5g; Sodium 24mg.

Crispy mango stacks with raspberry coulis

The mango and raspberries supercharge this stunning dessert with antioxidants. Filo pastry is a far healthier alternative to short crust or puff pastry because it is so much lower in fat. There is no added sugar, but if the raspberries are a little sharp, you may prefer to add a pinch of sugar to the purée.

Serves 4

3 filo pastry sheets, thawed
   if frozen
50g/2oz/¼ cup butter, melted
2 small ripe mangoes
115g/4oz/⅔ raspberries, thawed
   if frozen

1 Preheat the oven to 200°C/400°F/ Gas 6. Lay the filo sheets on a clean work surface and cut out four 10cm/4in rounds from each.

2 Brush each round with the melted butter and lay the rounds on two baking sheets. Bake for 5 minutes, or until crisp and golden. Place on wire racks to cool.

3 Peel the mangoes, remove the stones (pits) and cut the flesh into thin slices. Blend the raspberries in a food processor with 45ml/3 tbsp water to make a purée. Place a pastry round on each of four plates. Top with a quarter of the mango and drizzle with raspberry purée. Repeat until all the ingredients are used, finishing with a layer of mango and a dash of purée.

Crispy mango stacks: Energy 186Kcal/779kJ; Protein 2.2g; Carbohydrate 21.7g, of which sugars 11.9g; Fat 10.7g, of which saturates 6.7g; Cholesterol 27mg; Calcium 36mg; Fibre 3.1g; Sodium 79mg.

Pomegranate jewelled cheesecake

This whisked cheesecake is lighter in texture than most, and subtly flavoured with orange juice and coconut cream. The polyphenol-rich pomegranate topping offers a spectacular colour as well as providing cardioprotective benefits.

Serves 8

225g/8oz oat biscuits (cookies)
75g/3oz/⅓ cup unsalted butter, melted

For the filling
45ml/3 tbsp orange juice
15ml/1 tbsp powdered gelatine
250g/9oz/generous 1 cup mascarpone cheese
200g/7oz/scant 1 cup full-fat soft cheese
75g/3oz/¾ cup icing (confectioner's) sugar, sifted
200ml/7fl oz/scant 1 cup coconut cream
2 egg whites

For the topping
2 pomegranates, peeled and seeds separated
grated rind and juice of 1 orange
30ml/2 tbsp caster (superfine) sugar
15ml/1 tbsp arrowroot, mixed to a paste with 30ml/2 tbsp Kirsch
a few drops of red food colouring (optional)

1 Grease a 23cm/9in springform cake tin (pan). Crumb the biscuits in a food processor or blender, or by placing in a strong plastic bag and crushing them with a rolling pin. Add the melted butter and process briefly to combine. Spoon the mixture into the prepared tin and press it down firmly, then chill.

2 For the filling, pour the orange juice into a heatproof bowl, sprinkle the gelatine on top and set aside for 5 minutes until spongy. Place the bowl in a pan of hot water and stir until the gelatine has dissolved.

3 In a bowl, beat together both cheeses and the icing sugar, then gradually beat in the coconut cream. Whisk the egg whites in a grease-free bowl to soft peaks. Quickly stir the melted gelatine into the coconut mixture and fold in the egg whites. Pour over the biscuit base, level and chill until set.

COOK'S TIP
Cut the pomegranates in half and immerse in a bowl of water. Break the halves into quarters and remove the seeds with your fingers. The seeds will sink and the pith will float.

4 Make the cheesecake topping. Place the pomegranate seeds in a pan and add the orange rind and juice and caster sugar. Bring to the boil, then lower the heat, cover and simmer for 5 minutes. Add the arrowroot paste and heat, stirring constantly, until thickened. Stir in the food colouring, if using. Allow to cool, stirring occasionally.

5 Pour the glaze over the top of the set cheesecake, then chill. To serve, run a knife between the edge of the tin and the cheesecake, then remove the side of the tin.

Pomegranate cheesecake: Energy 407Kcal/1702kJ; Protein 8.2g; Carbohydrate 37.3g, of which sugars 26.1g; Fat 26.1g, of which saturates 15.2g; Cholesterol 56mg; Calcium 57mg; Fibre 1.1g; Sodium 336mg.

Red grape and cheese tartlets

Fruit and cheese is a natural combination in this delicious, low-sugar recipe. Choose the darkest red grapes available, as these contain the highest concentration of the cholesterol-reducing phytochemicals. To further reduce the fat content, you could use a low-fat cottage cheese.

2 Bake the tartlets for 10 minutes, remove the paper and beans, then return the cases to the oven for 5 minutes until golden and fully cooked. Remove the pastry cases from the tins and cool on a wire rack.

3 Meanwhile, beat the curd cheese, yogurt, vanilla extract and caster sugar in a bowl.

4 Divide the curd cheese mixture among the pastry cases. Smooth the surfaces flat and arrange the halved grapes on top.

5 To make the glaze, mix the arrowroot in a small pan with the apple juice. Bring to the boil, then remove from the heat. Cool, stirring occasionally.

6 Spoon the arrowroot over the grapes. Cool, then chill until set in the refrigerator before serving.

VARIATIONS
You can try using cranberry jelly or redcurrant jelly for the glaze. There will be no need to strain either of these. You can also vary the fruit topping, if you like. Try blackberries, blueberries, raspberries, sliced strawberries, kiwi fruit slices, banana slices or well-drained pineapple slices.

Makes 6

350g/12oz shortcrust pastry,
  thawed if frozen
225g/8oz/1 cup curd cheese or
  cottage cheese
150ml/¼ pint/⅔ cup natural
  (plain) bio-yogurt
2.5ml/½ tsp pure vanilla extract
15ml/1 tbsp caster (superfine) sugar
200g/7oz/2 cups red grapes,
  halved, seeded if necessary
5ml/1 tsp arrowroot
90ml/6 tbsp unsweetened
  apple juice

1 Preheat the oven to 200°C/400°F/ Gas 6. Roll out the pastry and line six deep 9cm/3½in tartlet tins (muffin pans). Prick the bases and line with baking parchment and baking beans.

Red grape tartlets: Energy 559kcal/2330kJ; Protein 10.4g; Carbohydrate 45.1g, of which sugars 19.7g; Fat 39.3g, of which saturates 23.9g; Cholesterol 164mg; Calcium 123mg; Fibre 1.3g; Sodium 331mg.

Blackcurrant tart

Blackcurrants grow in the wild and are cultivated throughout Europe and North America. This vitamin C-rich tart makes the most of these exquisite summer fruits, and is quick and easy to prepare. Serve with a generous dollop of low-fat crème fraîche.

Serves 4

115g/4oz plain (all-purpose) flour, plus 55g/2oz for the fruit mixture
55g/2oz butter, cut into chunks
30ml/2 tbsp cold water
500g/1¼lb blackcurrants
115g/4oz sugar
30ml/2 tbsp lemon juice

1 Pre-heat the oven to 200°C/400°F/ Gas 6. Lightly grease the base and edges of a 18cm/7in tart tin (pan).

2 In a large mixing bowl, rub the chunks of butter into the flour until the mix resembles breadcrumbs. Add the water, mix gently to form a dough, and place in a refrigerator for a few hours to rest.

3 In another bowl, gently mix together the fruit, sugar, lemon juice and flour.

4 Roll out the pastry to the correct size and line the tart tin (pan).

5 Spoon the fruit mixture into the tart tin and spread out evenly.

6 Bake in the centre of the oven for about 25 minutes.

7 Remove from the oven and cool. Serve with ice cream or low-fat crème fraîche.

VARIATION
Anthocyanin-rich elderberries are a great superfruit alternative to blackcurrants, but are harder to come by. In the UK, when in season, they grow in hedgerows. Collect as many as you can, then freeze them in batches so that you can use them all year round.

Blackcurrant tart: Energy 395Kcal/1669kJ; Protein 5g; Carbohydrate 71g, of which sugars 39g; Fat 12g, of which saturates 7g; Cholesterol 29mg; Calcium 140mg; Fibre 5.8g; Sodium 90mg.

Raspberry and almond tart

The antioxidant-rich, juicy, ripe raspberries and the LDL cholesterol-reducing almonds in this delicious recipe are a classic pairing for their taste as well as for their benefits to health. This stunning tart is ideal for serving at the end of a special lunch or at a dinner party.

Serves 4

200g/7oz shortcrust pastry
2 large (US extra large) eggs
75ml/2½fl oz/⅓ cup double (heavy) cream
50g/2oz/¼ cup caster (superfine) sugar
50g/2oz/½ cup ground almonds
20g/¾oz/4 tsp butter
350g/12oz/2 cups raspberries

1 Line a 20cm/8in flan tin (pan) with the pastry. Prick the base all over and leave to rest for at least 30 minutes. Preheat the oven to 200°C/400°F/Gas 6.

2 Put the eggs, cream, sugar and ground almonds in a bowl and whisk together briskly. Melt the butter and pour into the mixture, stirring to combine thoroughly.

3 Sprinkle the raspberries evenly over the pastry case. The ones at the top will appear through the surface, so keep them evenly spaced. You can also create a pattern with them.

4 Pour the egg and almond mixture over the top. Once again, ensure that it is spread evenly throughout the tart.

5 Bake in the preheated oven for 25 minutes. Serve warm or cold.

VARIATION
Peaches make a very attractive and tasty tart. Use 6 large, ripe peaches and remove the skin and stone (pit). Cut into slices and use in the same way as the raspberries above.

Raspberry and almond tart: Energy 548kcal/2284kJ; Protein 10.9g; Carbohydrate 41.7g, of which sugars 18.4g; Fat 38.8g, of which saturates 14.8g; Cholesterol 158mg; Calcium 128mg; Fibre 4.1g; Sodium 282mg.

Vanilla, honey and saffron pears

These sweet, juicy pears poached in a vanilla-, saffron- and lime-infused honey syrup make a truly elegant dessert. This low-fat dessert is good enough to eat on its own, but if you prefer, a serving of fresh-tasting bio-yogurt, crème fraîche or ice cream goes well.

Serves 4

150g/5oz/¾ cup caster (superfine) sugar
105ml/7 tbsp clear honey
5ml/1 tsp finely grated lime rind
a large pinch of saffron
2 vanilla pods (beans)
4 large, firm, ripe dessert pears
bio-yogurt, half-fat crème fraîche or ice cream, to serve

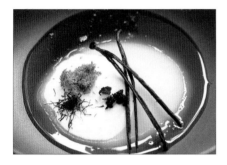

1 Place the caster sugar and honey in a medium, non-stick wok, then add the lime rind and the saffron. Using a small, sharp knife, split the vanilla pods in half and scrape the seeds into the wok, then add the vanilla pods as well.

2 Pour 500ml/17fl oz/scant 2¼ cups water into the wok and bring the mixture to the boil. Reduce the heat to low and simmer, stirring occasionally, as you prepare the pears.

3 Peel the pears, then add to the wok and gently turn in the syrup to coat evenly. Cover the wok and simmer gently for 12–15 minutes, turning the pears halfway through cooking, until they are just tender.

4 Lift the pears from the syrup using a slotted spoon and transfer to four serving bowls. Set aside.

5 Bring the syrup back to the boil and cook gently for about 10 minutes, or until reduced and thickened. Spoon the syrup over the pears and serve either warm or chilled with bio-yogurt, crème fraîche or ice cream.

VARIATIONS
For different syrup flavourings, try 10ml/2 tsp chopped fresh root ginger and 1–2 whole star anise in place of the saffron and vanilla, or 1 cinnamon stick, 3 cloves and 105ml/7 tbsp maple syrup instead of the spices and honey.

Vanilla and honey pears: Energy 283Kcal/1207kJ; Protein 0.8g; Carbohydrate 74.3g, of which sugars 74.3g; Fat 0.2g, of which saturates 0g; Cholesterol 0mg; Calcium 38mg; Fibre 3.3g; Sodium 10mg.

Winter fruit poached in mulled wine

A fabulous winter warmer, this dish combines fresh apples and pears with dried apricots and figs.
These are then cooked in a fragrant, spicy mulled wine until tender and intensely flavoured.
Boiling the wine will drive off some of the alcohol, but the healthy phytochemicals will remain.

3 Add the pears, figs and apricots to the pan and cook, covered, for 25 minutes, occasionally turning the fruit in the wine mixture. Add the sliced apples and cook for a further 12–15 minutes, until the fruit is tender.

4 Remove the fruit from the pan and discard the spices. Cook the wine mixture over a high heat until reduced and syrupy, then pour it over the fruit. Serve, decorated with the reserved orange rind, if wished.

Serves 4

300ml/½ pint/1¼ cups red wine
300ml/½ pint/1¼ cups fresh
  orange juice
finely grated rind and juice of
  1 orange
45ml/3 tbsp clear honey or barley
  malt syrup
1 cinnamon stick, broken in half
4 cloves
4 cardamom pods, split
2 pears, such as Comice or
  Williams (Bartlett), peeled, cored
  and halved
8 ready-to-eat dried figs
12 ready-to-eat dried unsulphured
  apricots
2 eating apples, peeled, cored and
  thickly sliced

1 Put the wine, the fresh and squeezed orange juice and half the orange rind in a pan with the honey or syrup and spices.

2 Bring to the boil, then reduce the heat and simmer for 2 minutes, stirring occasionally.

SUPERFOOD TIPS
• The combination of fresh and dried fruit ensures a healthy amount of vitamins and minerals, particularly vitamin C, beta-carotene, potassium and iron. The fruit is also rich in fibre.
• Cardamom and cinnamon soothe indigestion and, along with cloves, can offer relief from colds and coughs.

Poached winter fruit: Energy 494Kcal/2100kJ; Protein 7.3g; Carbohydrate 105.5g, of which sugars 105.5g; Fat 2.2g, of which saturates 0g; Cholesterol 0mg; Calcium 309mg; Fibre 14.6g; Sodium 85mg.

Apple and banana crumble

An old favourite, this crumble is sure to be popular with children and adults alike. While low in sugar and fat, this dessert remains rich in nutrients. The predominance of oats in the topping means that it will have a low glycaemic index and release energy slowly.

Serves 6

2 large cooking apples
2 large bananas
60ml/4 tbsp water
50g/2oz/¼ cup low-fat spread
30–45ml/2–3 tbsp pear and
    apple spread
25g/1oz/¼ cup wholemeal
    (whole-wheat) flour
115g/4oz/1 cup rolled oats
30ml/2 tbsp sunflower seeds
low-fat yogurt, to serve (optional)

3 Transfer the apple and banana mixture to a 18cm/7in baking dish and spread the oat crumble over the top. Bake for about 20 minutes or until the topping is golden brown. Serve warm or at room temperature, as it is or with low-fat yogurt.

1 Preheat the oven to 180°C/350°F/ Gas 4. Cut the apples into quarters, remove the cores, and then chop them into small pieces, leaving the skin on. Peel and slice the bananas. Mix the apples, bananas and water in a pan and cook until they become soft and pulpy.

2 Melt the low-fat spread with the pear and apple spread in a separate pan. Stir in the flour, oats and sunflower seeds and mix well.

Apple and banana crumble: Energy 207kcal/870kJ; Protein 5g; Carbohydrate 31g, of which sugars 14g; Fat 8g, of which saturates 2g; Cholesterol 1mg; Calcium 25mg; Fibre 3.8g; Sodium 58mg.

Grilled pineapple with papaya sauce

Warming fruit such as pineapple releases all the wonderful flavours and aromas, and chargrilling it gives them depth too. The fragrant papaya sauce complements the pineapple with its carotenoid rich orange-pink colour. Serve this dessert warm for a fragrant, fruity treat.

Serves 6

1 sweet pineapple
7.5ml/1½ tsp rapeseed oil,
   for greasing
2 pieces drained stem ginger in
   syrup, cut into fine matchsticks,
   plus 30ml/2 tbsp of the syrup
   from the jar
30ml/2 tbsp demerara
   (raw) sugar
pinch of ground cinnamon

For the sauce

1 ripe papaya, peeled and seeded
175ml/6fl oz/¾ cup apple juice

1 Peel the pineapple and cut spiral slices off the outside to remove the eyes. Cut the pineapple crossways into six 2.5cm/1in thick slices.

2 Line a baking sheet with foil, rolling up the sides to make a rim. Grease the foil with the oil.

3 Preheat the grill (broiler). Arrange the pineapple slices on the lined baking sheet. Top with the ginger matchsticks, sugar and cinnamon. Drizzle over the stem ginger syrup.

4 Grill (broil) for 5–7 minutes, or until the slices are golden and lightly charred on top.

5 Meanwhile, make the sauce. Cut a few slices from the papaya and set aside, then purée the rest with the apple juice in a food processor or blender.

6 Sieve (strain) the purée, then stir in any cooking juices from the pineapple. Serve the pineapple drizzled with the sauce and decorated with the papaya slices.

COOK'S TIPS
• You can use the papaya sauce made in this recipe as an accompaniment to savoury dishes, too. It tastes great with grilled chicken and game birds, as well as pork and lamb.
• Make the sauce in advance and freeze in an ice-cube tray. Defrost as needed.

Grilled pineapple with papaya sauce: Energy 92kcal/393kJ; Protein 1g; Carbohydrate 20g, of which sugars 20g; Fat 2g, of which saturates 0g; Cholesterol 0mg; Calcium 27mg; Fibre 1.8g; Sodium 4mg.

Summer berry crêpes

The delicate flavour of these crêpes contrasts beautifully with the nutrient-rich array of tangy berry fruits. This recipe very gently warms the summer fruits but retains their excellent vitamin content. Unsweetened apple juice makes a flavoursome alternative to sugar-water syrups.

Serves 4

115g/4oz/1 cup self-raising
   (self-rising) flour
1 large egg
300ml/½ pint/1¼ cups milk
a few drops of vanilla extract
15g/½oz/1 tbsp butter
15ml/1 tbsp sunflower oil
5ml/1 tsp icing (confectioners')
   sugar, for dusting

For the fruit
300ml/½ pint/1¼ cups
   unsweetened apple juice
juice of 2 oranges
thinly pared rind of ½ orange
350g/12oz/3 cups mixed
   summer berries

1 Preheat the oven to 150°C/300°F/Gas 2.

2 To make the crêpes, sift the flour into a large bowl and make a well in the centre. Break in the egg and gradually whisk in the milk to make a smooth batter. Stir in the vanilla extract. Set the batter aside in a cool place for up to half an hour.

3 Heat the butter and oil together in an 18cm/7in non-stick frying pan. Swirl to grease the pan, then pour off the excess fat into a small bowl.

4 If the batter has been left to stand, whisk it until smooth. Pour a little of the batter into the hot pan, swirling to coat the pan evenly.

5 Cook until the crêpe comes away from the sides and is golden underneath. Flip over the crêpe with a palette knife or metal spatula and cook the other side briefly until golden.

6 Slide the crêpe on to a plate, cover it with foil and keep warm in the oven. Make seven more crêpes.

7 To prepare the fruit, bring the apple juice to the boil in a pan. Boil until reduced by half. Add the orange juice and rind, and cook until slightly syrupy. Add the fruit and warm through.

8 Fold the pancakes into quarters and arrange two on each plate. Spoon some of the fruit over and dust lightly with icing sugar.

COOK'S TIP
Boiling unsweetened apple juice until it is reduced makes a good alternative to sugar-water syrups.

Summer berry crepes: Energy 260kcal/1099kJ; Protein 8g; Carbohydrate 45.9g, of which sugars 24.6g; Fat 3.5g, of which saturates 0.9g; Cholesterol 51mg; Calcium 235mg; Fibre 2.4g; Sodium 184mg.

Apple pudding

The understated vitamin C- and antioxidant-rich apple is at the heart of this very light soufflé-style pudding. This comforting, warm apple pudding is a perfect way to use up an autumnal glut, as the recipe works just as well with stewed or frozen apples.

2 Put the milk, butter and flour in a pan. Stirring constantly with a whisk, cook over a medium heat until the sauce thickens and comes to the boil. Let it bubble gently for 1–2 minutes, stirring well to make sure it does not stick and burn on the bottom of the pan. Pour into a bowl, add the sugar and vanilla extract, and then stir in the egg yolks.

3 In a separate bowl, whisk the egg whites until stiff peaks form. With a large metal spoon, fold the egg whites into the custard. Pour the custard mixture over the apples in the dish.

4 Put into the hot oven and cook for about 40 minutes until puffed up, deep golden brown and firm to the touch.

5 Serve immediately from the oven, before the soufflé-like topping begins to fall.

Serves 4

4 crisp eating apples
a little lemon juice
300ml/½ pint/1¼ cups milk
40g/1½oz/3 tbsp butter
40g/1½oz/⅓ cup plain
　(all-purpose) flour
25g/1oz/2 tbsp caster
　(superfine) sugar
2.5ml/½ tsp vanilla extract
2 eggs, separated

1 Preheat the oven to 200°C/400°F/ Gas 6. Butter a dish measuring 20–23cm/8–9in diameter and 5cm/2in deep. Peel, core and slice the apples and put in the dish.

VARIATIONS
Stewed fruit, such as cooking apples, plums, rhubarb or gooseberries sweetened with honey or sugar, would also make a good base for this pudding, as would fresh summer berries (blackberries, raspberries, redcurrants and blackcurrants).

Apple pudding: Energy 240kcal/1006kJ; Protein 7g; Carbohydrate 26.8g, of which sugars 19.2g; Fat 12.5g, of which saturates 6.8g; Cholesterol 121mg; Calcium 127mg; Fibre 1.9g; Sodium 131mg.

Caramel rice pudding with fruity compote

The fresh, fruity compote balances the sweetness of the caramel rice pudding and is quite wonderful. Dried apricots contain all of the concentrated goodness of their fresh counterparts and count as one of your five-a-day fruit portions, as well as being rich in calcium and iron.

Serves 4

1 vanilla pod (bean), split
300ml/½ pint/1¼ cups milk
300ml/½ pint/1¼ cups evaporated milk
50g/2oz/¼ cup short grain pudding rice

For the caramel
115g/4oz/½ cup granulated (white) sugar
90ml/6 tbsp water

For the compote
75g/3oz/6 tbsp caster (superfine) sugar
225g/8oz/1 cup ready-to-eat dried apricots
50g/2oz/½ cup whole blanched almonds
a few drops bitter almond extract, optional

1 Preheat the oven to 150°C/300°F/ Gas 2. To make the caramel, put the sugar and half the water in a heavy pan. Leave over a low heat, without stirring, until the sugar has dissolved and the liquid is clear. Increase the heat and gently boil until the liquid turns a caramel colour. Remove the pan from the heat, stand back and add the remaining water – take care as it will hiss and splutter.

2 Return the pan to a low heat and stir to dissolve the hardened pieces of caramel. Take the caramel off the heat and leave to cool for 2 minutes.

3 To make the rice pudding, put the split vanilla pod, milk and evaporated milk into a pan and bring slowly to the boil. Stir in the rice and cooled caramel, bring back to the boil, then pour into a shallow 900ml/1½ pint/ 3¾ cup ovenproof dish.

4 Bake the pudding for about 3 hours, or until a brown skin forms on top and the rice beneath is cooked and creamy.

5 Meanwhile, make the compote. Put the caster sugar and 300ml/½ pint/1¼ cups water in a pan and heat until the sugar has dissolved. Add the apricots, then cover and simmer for 20 minutes, until very soft. Stir in the almonds and extract, if using. Leave to cool, then chill.

6 Serve the rice pudding warm, with the cooled apricot and almond compote spooned on top.

COOK'S TIP
If you don't like the skin, you can simmer the rice pudding on top of the hob for about an hour rather than baking it in the oven.

Caramel rice pudding: Energy 545Kcal/2304kJ; Protein 15g; Carbohydrate 92g, of which sugars 81g; Fat 16g, of which saturates 6g; Cholesterol 30mg; Calcium 384mg; Fibre 4.5g; Sodium 180mg.

Dark chocolate and prune cake

This dark, cocoa rich cake is high in soluble fibre, which is good for gut health. It is also quite high in sugar, but this comes from the prunes and not from added sugar, so its energy will be released slowly, contributing to a lower glycaemic index. It is also gluten-free.

2 Mix the low-fat spread and prunes in a food processor. Process until light and fluffy, then scrape into a bowl.

3 Gradually fold in the melted chocolate and the eggs, alternately with the flour mixture. Beat in the soya milk.

4 Spoon the mixture into the cake tin, level the surface with a spoon, then bake for 20–30 minutes, or until the cake is firm to the touch. Leave to cool on a wire rack.

COOK'S TIP
For best results, use dark (bittersweet) chocolate with a high proportion of cocoa solids (70 per cent).

VARIATION
Try using ready-to-eat apricots in place of the prunes.

Makes a 20cm/8in cake

300g/11oz dark (bittersweet)
   chocolate
150g/5oz/⅔ cup low-fat spread
200g/7oz/generous 1 cup ready-to-
   eat stoned (pitted) prunes,
   quartered
3 eggs, beaten
150g/5oz/1¼ cups gram flour,
   sifted with 10ml/2 tsp baking
   powder
120ml/4fl oz/¼ cup soya milk

1 Preheat the oven to 180°C/350°F/ Gas 4. Grease and base-line a deep 20cm/8in round cake tin (pan). Melt the chocolate in a heatproof bowl over a pan of hot water.

Dark chocolate and prune cake: Energy 3173kcal/13294kJ; Protein 65g; Carbohydrate 376.8g, of which sugars 259.8g; Fat 166.1g, of which saturates 72.6g; Cholesterol 598mg; Calcium 537mg; Fibre 23.6g; Sodium 1268mg.

Apple and cinnamon cake

This cake is firm and moist, with pieces of apple peeking through the top. Keeping the apple skins on helps to increase the fibre content of the cake. The skins also retain the highest concentration of nutrients. This classic combination of apple with cinnamon is simply scrumptious.

Serves 6–8

375g/13oz/3¼ cups self-raising
   (self-rising) flour
3–4 large cooking apples, or
   cooking and eating apples
10ml/2 tsp ground cinnamon
500g/1¼lb/2½ cups caster
   (superfine) sugar
4 eggs, lightly beaten
250ml/8fl oz/1 cup vegetable oil
120ml/4fl oz/½ cup orange juice
10ml/2 tsp vanilla extract
2.5ml/½ tsp salt

3 In a separate bowl, beat the eggs together with the remaining sugar, the vegetable oil, orange juice and vanilla extract until all the ingredients are well combined. Sift in the remaining flour and salt, then stir into the mixture.

4 Pour two-thirds of the mixture into the tin and top with one-third of the apples. Pour over the rest of the cake mixture and top with the rest of the apples. Bake for 1 hour, or until golden brown. Cool in the tin to allow the juices to soak in. Cut into squares.

1 Preheat the oven to 180°C/350°F/ Gas 4. Grease a 30 × 38cm/12 × 15in square cake tin (pan) and dust with a little of the flour. Core and thinly slice the apples, but do not peel.

2 Put the sliced apples in a bowl, and mix with the cinnamon and 75ml/ 5 tbsp of the sugar.

SUPERFOOD TIP
Cinnamon can help to lower 'bad' LDL cholesterol.

COOK'S TIP
This recipe uses orange juice instead of milk, which makes it ideal for those that suffer from lactose intolerance.

Apple cake: Energy 653Kcal/2751kJ; Protein 7.8g; Carbohydrate 105.4g, of which sugars 70.6g; Fat 25.2g, of which saturates 3.4g; Cholesterol 95mg; Calcium 215mg; Fibre 2.1g; Sodium 210mg.

Green tea fruit loaf

This is a fabulous all-in-one, low-fat loaf cake. Use your favourite dried-fruit mix in this and make sure it is all well chopped to keep the cake light and moist. Soaking the fruit in the green tea adds to the antioxidant power of this delicious recipe.

Makes 1 loaf

300ml/10fl oz green tea (made up
   with 3 green tea bags)
250g/9oz dried fruit – any or a
   combination of raisins, sultanas
   (golden raisins), mixed peel,
   apricots and dates
225g/8oz self-raising
   (self-rising) flour
1 egg beaten
115g/4oz soft dark brown sugar
1 tbsp water (optional)

1 Make up the green tea using boiling water and soak the dried fruit in it for at least 4 hours.

2 Pre-heat oven 160°C/325°F/ Gas 3. Grease your loaf tin (pan) and line with baking parchment.

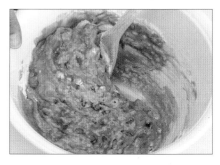

3 Add the flour, beaten egg and sugar into the soaked fruit and stir thoroughly. Add the water if it is too dry.

4 Pour into the loaf tin and bake in the centre of the oven for 1 hour. Check that the centre of the cake is cooked by inserting a skewer into the middle of the cake. The loaf is cooked when the skewer comes out clean.

5 Remove the cooked loaf from oven and let cool for 5 minutes. Turn out of the tin and leave to cool completely.

> **SUPERFOOD TIP**
> Add your favourite chopped nuts and seeds to the batter to boost the nutrient content.

Green tea fruit loaf: Energy 1918Kcal/8183kJ; Protein 34g; Carbohydrate 457g, of which sugars 290g; Fat 10g, of which saturates 2g; Cholesterol 232mg; Calcium 1070mg; Fibre 12.5g: Sodium 1051mg.

Goji berry and cinnamon muffins

These lovely muffins are high in fibre that keeps the glycaemic index down, and this helps you to feel fuller for longer. The soaking of the nutrient-packed goji berries and raisins keeps them succulent, and makes them a delight to eat. They are a tasty treat for any time of the day.

Makes 12

55g/2oz goji berries
55g/2oz raisins
100ml/3fl oz apple juice
115g/4oz melted butter
115g/4oz golden caster
   (superfine) sugar
150ml/4fl oz milk
2 eggs, beaten
125g/4¼oz self-raising
   (self-rising) flour
125g/4¼oz wholemeal
   (whole-wheat) self-raising
   (self-rising) flour
10ml/2 tsp baking powder
10ml/2 tsp ground cinnamon
5ml/1 tsp vanilla extract
25g/1oz porridge oats

1 Pre-heat the oven to 190°C/375°F/ Gas 5. Grease a muffin tin (pan) and line with muffin cases.

2 Soak the goji berries and raisins in the apple juice.

3 In a jug (pitcher), mix the melted butter, sugar, milk and beaten eggs.

4 In a large bowl, sift together the two flours, baking powder and cinnamon, add the oats.

5 Make a well in the centre and pour in the jug of liquid. Mix together and fold in the fruit.

6 Spoon into the muffin cases, sprinkle over the oats and place in the centre of the oven for 20 minutes.

7 Ensure that that a skewer comes out clean before removing from the oven to cool.

Goji berry muffins: Energy 233Kcal/979kJ; Protein 5g; Carbohydrate 37g, of which sugars 20g; Fat 10g, of which saturates 6g; Cholesterol 63mg; Calcium 97mg; Fibre 2g; Sodium 200mg.

Beetroot and bitter chocolate muffins

Unusual in baking, freshly cooked beetroot contrasts well with the intense cocoa flavour of bitter chocolate. Both beetroot and cocoa are heart-healthy, as they keep the blood vessels strong and 'bad' cholesterol levels in check, and are rich in antioxidants.

3 Whisk the beetroot into the melted chocolate and butter with the eggs.

4 Fold in the sifted flour, baking powder and sugar. Do not overmix. Spoon the batter into the prepared tin. Dust with the rye flour.

5 Bake for 25 minutes until risen and springy to the touch. Leave to cool for 5 minutes, then transfer to a wire rack to go completely cold.

6 To make the ganache topping, bring the cream to the boil. Remove from the heat and leave for 1 minute. Break the chocolate into the hot cream. Stir until the chocolate melts and the mixture is smooth.

7 Add the butter and continue to stir until the mixture looks glossy. Use it immediately for a topping.

8 Spread the top of each muffin with the chocolate ganache and eat fresh.

Makes 10

115g/4oz dark (bittersweet) chocolate (70% cocoa solids)
115g/4oz/½ cup butter
250g/9oz beetroot (beets), cooked, peeled and grated
3 eggs, lightly beaten
225g/8oz/2 cups self-raising (self-rising) flour
2.5ml/½ tsp baking powder
200g/7oz/1 cup caster (superfine) sugar
20–30ml/1½–2 tbsp rye flour

For the ganache topping
75ml/2½ fl oz/⅓ cup double (heavy) cream
175g/6oz dark (bittersweet) chocolate (70% cocoa solids)
25g/1oz/2 tbsp butter

1 Preheat the oven to 180°C/350°F/ Gas 4. Lightly grease the cups of a muffin tin (pan) or line them with paper cases.

2 Melt the chocolate and butter in a large heatproof bowl set over a pan of barely simmering water. Stir occasionally. Remove from the heat once the mixture is fully melted.

COOK'S TIP
To cook beetroot, trim the stems 2.5cm/1in above the bulbs, taking care not to tear the skin. Put the beetroot in a pan of boiling water and boil for 1½ hours, until tender. Drain and cool, then nip off the stems and roots.

Beetroot and chocolate muffins: Energy 342kcal/1437kJ; Protein 5.4g; Carbohydrate 50g, of which sugars 30.2g; Fat 14.8g, of which saturates 8.7g; Cholesterol 85mg; Calcium 112mg; Fibre 1.5g; Sodium 218mg.

Raisin and bran muffins

Low in fat and in sugar, these delicious muffins are made with a combination of wholemeal flour, bran and juicy raisins, and are flavoured with cinnamon. Their low glycaemic index makes them a perfect option for an on-the-go breakfast or a tasty mid-afternoon snack.

Makes 5

40g/1½oz/⅓ cup plain (all-purpose) flour
50g/2oz/½ cup wholemeal (whole-wheat) flour
7.5ml/1½ tsp bicarbonate of soda (baking soda)
5ml/1 tsp ground cinnamon
30g/1oz/⅓ cup bran
85g/3oz raisins
65g/2½oz/⅓ cup soft dark brown sugar
50g/2oz/¼ cup caster (superfine) sugar
1 egg, beaten
250ml/8fl oz/1 cup buttermilk
juice of ½ lemon
50g/2oz/4 tbsp butter, melted

1 Preheat the oven to 200°C/400°F/ Gas 6.

2 Grease the cups of a muffin tin (pan) or line them with paper cases.

3 In a mixing bowl, sift together the flours, bicarbonate of soda and cinnamon.

4 Add the bran, raisins and sugars and stir until blended.

5 In another bowl, mix together the egg, buttermilk, lemon juice and melted butter. Add the buttermilk mixture to the dry ingredients, and whisk lightly and quickly until just moistened.

6 Spoon the mixture into the prepared paper cases, filling the cups almost to the top. Half-fill any empty cups with water so that the muffins bake evenly.

7 Bake for 15–20 minutes. Leave to stand for 5 minutes, before turning out on to a wire rack to cool. Serve warm or at room temperature. Store in an airtight container for up to 3 days.

> **COOK'S TIP**
> If buttermilk is not available, add 10ml/2 tsp lemon juice or vinegar to milk. Let the mixture stand and curdle, about 30 minutes.

Raisin and bran muffins: Energy 89kcal/374kJ; Protein 2g; Carbohydrate 13.4g, of which sugars 8.9g; Fat 3.4g, of which saturates 1.9g; Cholesterol 20mg; Calcium 34mg; Fibre 1.1g; Sodium 36mg.

Date and muesli slice

Full of oats, seeds, dates, raisins and bio-yogurt, this is a supernutrient-packed treat. The light lemon-flavoured icing tops these scrumptious, low-fat muesli bars, making them the perfect mid-morning pick-me-up, or a welcome addition to a lunchbox or picnic.

Makes 12–16

175g/6oz/¾ cup light muscovado (brown) sugar
175g/6oz/1 cup ready-to-eat dried dates, chopped
115g/4oz/1 cup self-raising (self-rising) flour
50g/2oz/½ cup muesli (granola)
30ml/2 tbsp sunflower seeds
15ml/1 tbsp poppy seeds
30ml/2 tbsp sultanas (golden raisins)
150ml/¼ pint/⅔ cup natural (plain) low-fat bio-yogurt
1 egg, beaten
200g/7oz/1¾ cups icing (confectioners') sugar, sifted
lemon juice
15–30ml/1–2 tbsp pumpkin seeds

1 Preheat the oven to 180°C/350°F/Gas 4. Line a 28 x 18cm/11 x 7in shallow baking tin (pan) with baking parchment. Mix together all the ingredients except the icing sugar, lemon juice and pumpkin seeds.

2 Spread the mixture evenly in the tin and bake for about 25 minutes, until golden brown. Allow to cool.

3 To make the topping, put the icing sugar in a bowl and stir in just enough lemon juice to give a thick, spreading consistency.

4 Spread the lemon topping over the baked mixture and sprinkle generously with pumpkin seeds. Leave to set before cutting into squares or bars.

Date and muesli slice: Energy 176kcal/749kJ; Protein 3g; Carbohydrate 38.7g, of which sugars 31.3g; Fat 2.1g, of which saturates 0.3g; Cholesterol 12mg; Calcium 72mg; Fibre 1.1g; Sodium 45mg.

Almond, orange and carrot bars

Carrot cake becomes a cookie bar in this more portable version, and is a great way to add to the fruit and vegetable count of lunchboxes. The almonds and walnuts also add some essential fatty acids into the mix, as well as B vitamins and a host of minerals.

Makes 16

75g/3oz/6 tbsp unsalted
   butter, softened
50g/2oz/¼ cup caster (superfine)
   sugar
150g/5oz/1¼ cups wholemeal
   (whole-wheat) flour
finely grated rind of 1 orange

For the filling
90g/3½oz/7 tbsp unsalted
   butter, diced
75g/3oz/scant ½ cup caster
   (superfine) sugar
2 eggs
2.5ml/½ tsp almond extract
175g/6oz/1½ cups ground almonds
1 large cooked carrot, finely
   chopped

For the topping
175g/6oz/¾ cup cream cheese
30–45ml/2–3 tbsp chopped
   walnuts

1 Preheat the oven to 190°C/375°F/ Gas 5. Lightly grease a 28 x 18cm/ 11 x 7in shallow baking tin (pan).

2 Put the butter, caster sugar, flour and orange rind into a bowl and rub together until the mixture resembles coarse breadcrumbs. Add water, a teaspoon at a time, to mix to a firm but not sticky dough. Roll out on a lightly floured surface and use to line the base of the tin.

3 To make the filling, cream the butter and sugar together. Beat in the eggs and almond essence. Stir in the ground almonds and the finely chopped carrot. Spread the mixture over the dough base and bake for about 25 minutes until firm in the centre and golden brown. Leave to cool in the tin.

4 To make the topping, beat the cream cheese until smooth and spread it over the cooled, cooked filling. Swirl with a small palette knife or metal spatula, and sprinkle with the chopped walnuts. Cut into bars with a sharp knife.

Almond, orange and carrot bars: Energy 85Kcal/355kJ; Protein 1.4g; Carbohydrate 5.3g, of which sugars 2.9g; Fat 6.6g, of which saturates 3g; Cholesterol 18mg; Calcium 20mg; Fibre 0.4g; Sodium 34mg.

Fruit and millet treacle cookies

Brimming with dried fruit, these tasty little cookies are very quick and simple to make. The highly nutritious millet flakes give them a lovely crumbly texture and they are sure to be popular with the whole family, as a quick on-the-go snack or served with tea.

Makes 25–30

90g/3½oz/7 tbsp margarine
150g/5oz/⅔ cup light muscovado (brown) sugar
30ml/2 tbsp black treacle (molasses)
1 egg
150g/5oz1¼ cups self-raising (self-rising) flour
50g/2oz/½ cup millet flakes
50g/2oz/½ cup almonds, chopped
200g/7oz/generous 1 cup luxury mixed dried fruit

COOK'S TIP
Millet flakes can be replaced with rolled oats, wheat flakes or barley flakes.

1 Preheat the oven to 190°C/375°F/ Gas 5. Line two large baking sheets with baking parchment.

2 Put the margarine, muscovado sugar, treacle and egg in a large bowl and beat together until well combined. (The mixture should be soft and fluffy.)

3 Stir in the flour, millet flakes, almonds and dried fruit. Put tablespoonfuls of the mixture well apart on to the prepared baking sheet.

4 Bake for about 15 minutes until brown. Leave on the baking sheets for a few minutes, then transfer to a wire rack to cool completely.

Fruit and millet treacle cookies: Energy 99kcal/416kJ; Protein 1.4g; Carbohydrate 15.7g, of which sugars 10.6g; Fat 3.8g, of which saturates 1.2g; Cholesterol 7mg; Calcium 26mg; Fibre 0.5g; Sodium 33mg.

Psyllium, ginger and chocolate chip cookies

You wouldn't believe that these cookies were stacked full of fibre from the cardioprotective, cholesterol-reducing psyllium seed husk. The ginger pieces and dark chocolate are a tasty combination that makes these cookies a real tea-time treat.

Makes 8

rapeseed oil, for greasing
50g/2oz olive oil-based spread
85g/3oz golden caster
   (superfine) sugar
115g/4oz plain (all-purpose) flour
1 egg, beaten
25g/1oz psyllium fibre
2.5ml/½ tsp baking powder
2.5ml/½ tsp vanilla extract
50g/2oz plain chocolate chips
50g/2oz crystallized ginger,
   chopped
2–3 tbsp milk

1 Preheat the oven to 180°C/350°F/ Gas 4. Lightly grease a large 20cm/8in baking sheet.

2 Using a wooden spoon, soften the olive oil spread and sugar together in a bowl until creamy and pale. Sift the flour into the mixing bowl and add the beaten egg. Mix well.

3 Stir in the psyllium fibre, baking powder and vanilla extract, followed by the chocolate chips and ginger.

4 Gradually add the milk until the mixture is soft and spoonable. Spoon eight balls on to the baking sheet, leaving enough space between each to allow them to spread. Gently flatten each into a round.

5 Bake in the centre of the oven for 15 minutes. Leave on the baking sheet to cool for a few minutes, then lift off the sheet and transfer to a wire rack. Leave the cookies to cool completely before eating.

Psylliium and chocolate chip cookies: Energy 193Kcal/811kJ; Protein 3g; Carbohydrate 31g, of which sugars 17g; Fat 7g, of which saturates 2g; Cholesterol 30mg; Calcium 45mg; Fibre 3.0g; Sodium 90mg.

Herby seeded oatcakes

The thyme and sunflower seeds in this traditional recipe add to the heart-healthy credentials of the oats by reducing cholesterol levels. Their triangular shape and sunflower-seed topping gives them an interesting rustic appearance, perfect for a cheese board or simply to snack on.

Makes 32

175g/6oz/1½ cups plain
  wholemeal (whole-wheat) flour
175g/6oz/1½ cups fine oatmeal
5ml/1 tsp salt
1.5ml/¼ tsp bicarbonate of soda
  (baking soda)
75g/3oz/6 tbsp white vegetable
  fat (shortening)
15ml/1 tbsp fresh thyme leaves,
  chopped
30ml/2 tbsp sunflower seeds
rolled oats, for sprinkling

1 Preheat the oven to 150°C/300°F/ Gas 2. Sprinkle two ungreased, non-stick baking sheets with rolled oats and set aside.

2 Put the flour, oats, salt and soda in a bowl and rub in the fat until the mixture resembles fine breadcrumbs. Stir in the thyme.

3 Add just enough cold water (about 90–105ml/6–7 tbsp) to the dry ingredients to mix to a stiff, but not sticky, dough.

4 Gently knead the dough on a lightly floured surface until smooth, then cut roughly in half and roll out one piece on a lightly floured surface to make a 23–25cm/9–10in round.

5 Sprinkle sunflower seeds over the dough and press them in with the rolling pin. Cut into triangles and arrange on one of the baking sheets. Repeat with the remaining dough. Bake for 45–60 minutes, until crisp but not brown. Cool on wire racks.

Herby seeded oatcakes: Energy 62Kcal/259kJ; Protein 1.6g; Carbohydrate 7.7g, of which sugars 0.2g; Fat 3g, of which saturates 0.9g; Cholesterol 0mg; Calcium 6mg; Fibre 0.9g; Sodium 21mg.

Sultana and walnut bread

Featuring the cardioprotective might of the walnut, this bread is versatile and delicious with sweet or savoury foods. Serve with soups or salads or with a little jam for afternoon tea. Try substituting the walnuts with chopped brazil nuts for a selenium boost.

Makes 1 loaf

300g/11oz/2¾ cups strong
   white bread flour
2.5ml/½ tsp salt
15ml/1 tbsp butter
7.5ml/1½ tsp easy-blend
   dried yeast
115g/4oz/scant 1 cup sultanas
   (golden raisins)
75g/3oz/½ cup walnuts or brazil
   nuts, roughly chopped
melted butter, for brushing

1 Sift the flour and salt into a bowl, cut in the butter with a knife, then stir in the yeast.

2 Gradually add 175ml/6 fl oz/¾ cup tepid water to the flour mixture, stirring with a spoon at first, then gathering the dough together with your hands.

3 Turn the dough out on to a floured surface and knead for about 10 minutes until smooth and elastic.

4 Knead the sultanas and walnuts or brazil nuts into the dough until they are evenly distributed. Shape into a rough oval, place on a lightly oiled baking sheet and cover with oiled clear film (plastic wrap). Leave to rise in a warm place for 1–2 hours, until doubled in bulk. Preheat the oven to 220°C/425°F/Gas 7.

5 Uncover the loaf and bake for 10 minutes, then reduce the oven temperature to 190°C/375°F/Gas 5 and bake for a further 20–25 minutes.

6 Transfer to a wire rack, brush with melted butter and cover with a dish towel. Cool before slicing.

Sultana bread: Energy 1971kcal/8303kJ; Protein 50g; Carbohydrate 308g, of which sugars 86g; Fat 68g, of which saturates 13g; Cholesterol 32mg; Calcium 569mg; Fibre 23.2g; Sodium 1111mg.

Wholemeal sunflower bread

Adding seeds to bread is a wonderful way of making it more nutritious and interesting. Sunflower seeds give a nutty crunchiness to this high-fibre wholemeal loaf, which tastes delicious served simply with a chunk of cheese and lycopene-rich tomato chutney.

Makes 1 loaf

450g/1lb/4 cups wholemeal
  (whole-wheat) flour
2.5ml/½ tsp easy-blend dried yeast
2.5ml/½ tsp salt
50g/2oz/½ cup sunflower seeds,
  plus extra for sprinkling

SUPERFOOD TIP
You can try adding 10ml/2 tbsp of honey to give a sweet note to this scrumptious bread.

1 Grease and lightly flour a 450g/1lb loaf tin (pan). Mix together the flour, yeast, salt and sunflower seeds in a large bowl. Make a well in the centre and gradually stir in 300ml/½ pint/1¼ cups warm water. Mix vigorously with a wooden spoon to form a soft, sticky dough.

2 Cover the bowl with a damp dish towel and leave the dough to rise in a warm place for 45–50 minutes, or until doubled in bulk.

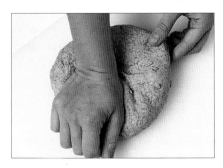

3 Preheat the oven to 200°C/400°F/ Gas 6. Turn out the dough on to a floured work surface and knead for 10 minutes – it will still be quite sticky.

4 Form the dough into a rectangle and put in the tin. Sprinkle sunflower seeds. Cover with a damp dish towel and leave to rise for 15 minutes.

5 Bake for 40–45 minutes, until golden. Leave for 5 minutes, then turn out of the tin and leave to cool.

Wholemeal bread: Energy 1686Kcal/7136kJ; Protein 67g; Carbohydrate 296.9g, of which sugars 10.3g; Fat 33.6g, of which saturates 3.6g; Cholesterol 0mg; Calcium 226mg; Fibre 43.5g; Sodium 998mg.

Rosemary and rock salt focaccia

Enriched with monounsaturate-rich black olives and olive oil and flavoured with rosemary and garlic, this popular Italian bread makes it a truly Mediterranean treat and a perfect accompaniment to a salad. Rosemary is supposed to be good for the memory, so remember not to overdo the salt.

Makes 1 loaf

225g/8oz/2 cups unbleached plain
  (all-purpose) flour, sifted
2.5ml/½ tsp salt
7g/¼oz sachet easy-blend
  dried yeast
4 garlic cloves, finely chopped
2 sprigs of rosemary, leaves
  removed and chopped
10 black olives, stoned (pitted)
  and roughly chopped (optional)
15ml/1 tbsp olive oil

For the topping
90ml/6 tbsp olive oil
sprinkling of rock salt
1 sprig of rosemary, leaves removed

1 Mix together the flour, salt, yeast, garlic, rosemary and olives, if using, in a large bowl. Make a well in the centre and add the olive oil and 150ml/¼ pint/⅔ cup warm water. Mix well until a soft dough is formed.

2 Turn out the dough on to a floured work surface and knead for 10–15 minutes. Put the dough in an oiled bowl and cover with oiled clear film or a dish towel. Leave to rise in a warm place for 45 minutes, until the dough has doubled in bulk.

3 Turn out the dough and knead lightly again. Roll out to an oval shape, about 1cm/½in thick. Put the dough on a greased baking sheet, cover loosely with oiled clear film (plastic wrap) or a dish towel and leave in a warm place for 25–30 minutes to rise again.

4 Preheat the oven to 200°C/400°F/ Gas 6. Make indentations with your fingertips all over the top of the bread. Drizzle two-thirds of the olive oil over the top, then sprinkle with the rock salt and rosemary. Bake for 25 minutes until golden.

5 When ready, the bread will sound hollow when tapped underneath. Transfer to a wire rack, and spoon the remaining olive oil over the top.

SUPERFOOD TIP
Olives are a good source of iron and the antioxidant vitamin E.

Rosemary focaccia: Energy 1699Kcal/7177kJ; Protein 37.8g; Carbohydrate 311g, of which sugars 9.7g; Fat 42.3g, of which saturates 6.1g; Cholesterol 0mg; Calcium 568mg; Fibre 13.1g; Sodium 14mg.

Tofu and strawberry whizz

This energizing blend is bursting with goodness. Not only is tofu a perfect source of protein, it is also rich in minerals. With seeds and strawberries, this creamy blend makes a delicious alternative to an after-meal dessert. You can make it in advance and store in the refrigerator for later in the day.

Serves 2

250g/9oz firm tofu
200g/7oz/1¾ cups strawberries
45ml/3 tbsp pumpkin or sunflower seeds, plus a few extra for sprinkling
juice of 2 large oranges

1 Roughly chop the tofu, then hull and roughly chop the strawberries. Reserve a few strawberry chunks.

VARIATIONS
Almost any fruit can be used instead of strawberries. Mangoes, bananas and peaches blend well.

2 Put all the ingredients in a blender or food processor and blend until completely smooth, scraping the mixture down from the side of the bowl, if necessary.

3 Pour the smoothie into tumblers and sprinkle the top with extra seeds and a few strawberry chunks.

Creamy acai berry smoothie

The banana and bio-yogurt ingredients in this thick and creamy smoothie help to calm down the somewhat acidic flavour of the nutrient-rich acai berry juice. This recipe makes one glass of rich purple-coloured, detoxifying smoothie. Serve with blueberries for an extra nutrient punch.

Serves 1

100ml/3 fl oz acai berry juice
1 large ripe banana
150ml/5 fl oz bio-yogurt
a handful of blueberries, to serve

1 Place the acai berry juice, the banana and the bio-yogurt into a blender together.

2 Pulse all of the ingredients gently together until they reach a smooth consistency and serve immediately.

SUPERFOOD TIP
Acai berries are rich in potassium, anthocyanins, B vitamins and fibre, as well as omega-3 fatty acids.

Tofu and strawberry whizz: Energy 267kcal/1112kJ; Protein 15.7g; Carbohydrate 15.5g, of which sugars 11.2g; Fat 16.1g, of which saturates 1.7g; Cholesterol 0mg; Calcium 684mg; Fibre 2.5g; Sodium 17mg.
Creamy acai berry smoothie: Energy 307Kcal/1248kJ; Protein 9g; Carbohydrate 33g, of which sugars 31g; Fat 16g, of which saturates 10g; Cholesterol 25mg; Calcium 194mg; Fibre 0.7g; Sodium 100mg.

Green tea latte

This Asian twist on an Italian classic is a delightful, sweet beverage. The flavonoids in the green tea are thought to be responsible for its health benefits, and serving it with hot milk calms its flavour a little. You can use water instead of milk if you wish to enhance the green tea flavour.

Serves 4

1 litre/1¾ pints/4 cups milk
60ml/4 tbsp green tea powder
    or maacha
30ml/2 tbsp sugar
120ml/4fl oz/½ cup whipping
    cream (optional)
10ml/2 tsp caster (superfine) sugar
    or honey (optional)

1 Heat the milk in a pan over a low heat until it simmers gently. Add the green tea powder and sugar, and stir well.

2 Remove from the heat and pour the tea into a bowl or jug (pitcher). Leave to cool before chilling.

3 When ready to serve the tea, whisk the cream until it begins to thicken. Then add the caster sugar or honey and continue to whisk until the cream is light and fluffy.

4 Pour the chilled green tea into tall glasses and top with whipped cream. and a dusting of green tea powder.

Cardamom hot chocolate

Using dark chocolate instead of a chocolate powder is better as you get the goodness of the cocoa without the sugar. Cardamom is traditionally used to flavour milky drinks in the Middle East and is a wonderful partner for chocolate in this indulgent, soothing treat.

Serves 4

900ml/1½ pints/3¾ cups milk
2 cardamom pods, bruised
200g/7oz plain (semisweet)
    chocolate, broken into pieces

1 Put the milk in a pan with the cardamom pods and bring to the boil. Add the chocolate and whisk until melted.

2 Using a slotted spoon, remove the cardamom pods and discard. Pour the hot chocolate into heat-proof glasses, mugs or cups, and serve immediately.

Green tea latte: Energy 269kcal/1126kJ; Protein 9.2g; Carbohydrate 23g, of which sugars 23g; Fat 16.4g, of which saturates 10.3g; Cholesterol 46mg; Calcium 323mg; Fibre 0g; Sodium 116mg.
Cardamom hot chocolate: Energy 359Kcal/1567kJ: Protein 10g: Carbohydrate 42g of which sugars 42g; Fat 18g of which saturates 11g: Cholesterol 6mg: Calcium 127mg: Fibre 0g: Sodium 100mg.

Glossary

A

Alpha-linolenic acid – an omega-3 fatty acid found in some vegetables.

Acetylcholine – an important neurotransmitter in the brain, formed from choline, found in eggs, liver and wheatgerm.

Acidophilus (culture) – a specific strain of bacteria which helps with digestion.

Alginic acid – found in seaweed, can bind heavy metals and remove them from our body.

Allicin – active compound found in onions and garlic, reduces heart disease and cancer risk.

Amino acid – the basic building blocks used to make proteins.

Anthocyanin – pigments in vegetables and fruits, reduce cancer and heart disease risk.

Anthraquinone – a type of polyphenol found in rhubarb that has laxative effects in the body.

Antioxidants – inhibit the oxidation and potential damage to body cells by free radicals.

Ascorbic acid – also known as vitamin C, found in most fruit and vegetables, essential for healthy skin and a strong immune system.

Atherosclerosis – a condition where the arteries become clogged with fatty deposits.

B

Beta-carophyllene – an essential oil with anti-inflammatory properties, found in basil

Beta-carotene (b-carotene) – an orange pigment found in carrots, mangoes, papayas and pumpkins, converted by the body into vitamin A.

Beta-cryptoxanthin – a red pigment found in egg yolks, papayas and orange rind, that can be converted in the body to vitamin A, which is essential for maintaining good eyesight.

Beta-glucan – a fibre found in oats, barley and mushrooms that helps reduce cholesterol levels.

Betalain – a red/orange pigment found in beetroot (beet) with strong antioxidant activity.

Bifidobacterium – bacteria found in bio-dairy products that contribute to a healthy gastrointestinal tract.

Bioavailability – a measure of how available a nutrient is for absorption and use by the body.

Bromelain – an enzyme found in pineapples that can break down protein and can have anti-inflammatory effects.

C

Calciferol – another name for vitamin D, found in dairy products, canned fish with bones and vegetable oils, it is essential for healthy bones.

Capsaicin – active compound found in chillies that can stimulate the release of endorphins.

Carnosic acid – a powerful antioxidant in rosemary, may have benefits for brain health.

Carotenoid – a large family of pigments found in plants and algae.

Catechin – a compound found in tea that has potent antioxidant activity.

Chlorophyll – a green pigment in plant cells, enables them to convert sunlight into energy.

Cholesterol – a substance made by the liver, used to make hormones, part of all cell tissues.

Cineole – a volatile oil in cardamom and eucalyptus, thought to alleviate congestion.

Citral – a volatile compound in lemongrass, lemon, lime and lemon balm with high antioxidant activity.

Conjugated Linoleic Acid (CLA) – forms of the fatty acid linoleic acid found in dairy products and the meat of ruminant animals.

Coumaric acid – compound found in peanuts, with a very high level of antioxidant activity.

Cruciferous – vegetables from the brassica family such as cabbage, sprouts, spinach, broccoli and kale. May reduce cancer risk.

Cyanocobalamin (or vitamin B12) – found in dairy foods, eggs and yeast, essential for a healthy nervous system and maintaining energy levels.

Cynarin – compound found in artichokes, may help in liver health and cholesterol metabolism.

D

Deoxyribonucleic acid (DNA) – found in the cells of all living things, forms chromosomes and genes.

Docosahexanoic acid (DHA) – a type of omega-3 fatty acid found in fish. Significant in the structure of the brain and of the retina in the eye.

E

Epicatechin – a very similar compound to catechin, found in cocoa and tea.

EPA (Eicosapentanoic acid) – a type of omega-3 fatty acid found in fish. Significant in the production of anti-inflammatory compounds.

Essential amino acid – a constituent of protein foods that cannot be made by the body.

Essential fatty acid – a constituent of fat that cannot be made by the body.

Eugenol – an oily liquid compound with antibacterial and antiviral properties, found in clove oil, nutmeg, cinnamon and basil.

F

FDA (Food and Drug Administration) – US agency for protecting and promoting public health.

Fisetin – a compound found in strawberries that may help improve brain function.

Flavonoids (or bioflavonoids) – large family of compounds found in plants that include many plant pigments, with potent antioxidant properties and are associated with the health benefits of tea, red wine and of fruit and vegetables.

Folate (or folic acid) – a B-vitamin found in wholegrains and green leafy vegetables, essential for healthy cell division especially in the foetus.

Free radicals – the potentially damaging agents found both naturally in the body and externally in cigarette smoke. Can cause cell damage.

G

Glycemic Index (GI) – a measure of how quickly energy is released in the body by food. One hundred is the highest and represents the fastest energy release from pure glucose. The lower the number the slower the energy release.

Gingerol – active compound in ginger with anti-nausea and anti-inflammatory properties.

Glucosinolate – sulphur-containing compounds found in brassica vegetables thought to be responsible for potential anti-cancer properties.

H

HDL (High Density Lipoprotein) – a compound sometimes known as 'good cholesterol' found in the blood that carries cholesterol back to the liver and removes it from the blood.

Hesperidin – a type of flavonoid found in citrus fruits that can help strengthen blood vessels and may reduce heart disease risk.

Hypercholesterolaemia – a genetic condition whereby the blood cholesterol levels are very high.

I

Insoluble fibre – the type of fibre that is able to absorb water but not dissolve in it, helping bulk and good intestinal health.

Inulin – a type of soluble fibre found in Jerusalem artichokes that has probiotic properties.

Isoflavones – compounds found in soya and alfalfa with phytoestrogen properties and the potential to reduce circulating cholesterol levels.

L

LDL (Low density Lipoprotein) – the form of cholesterol that stays in the blood and is sometimes known as 'bad cholesterol'. High LDL levels increase the risk of heart disease.

Lectins – toxic substance in red kidney beans that is removed by boiling the dried beans vigorously.

Lentinan – the specific beta-glucan found in mushrooms with anti-tumour properties.

Lignin – a substance found in plant cell walls that acts as a type of dietary fibre.

Lipid – an alternative word for fat or oil.

Lutein – a yellow-pigmented compound found in mangoes and pumpkins that aids vision and may reduce risk of age-related macular degeneration.

Lycopene – a red-pigmented carotene that does not have vitamin A properties like other carotenes. It is found in tomatoes, pink grapefruit and watermelon, can help reduce prostate cancer risk.

M/N

Mono-unsaturated fat – a type of fat found in olive oil, avocado and nuts that can reduce heart disease risk.

Nutrient – a chemical that the body needs in order to live and grow and maintain itself. Food is our main source of nutrients.

O

ORAC (oxygen radical absorption capacity) – a way of measuring how powerful the antioxidant capacity of a food or substance is. The higher the ORAC score the more potent the activity.

Omega-3 fat – a type of fat found in oily fish, walnuts, rapeseed and soya, that has many health benefits, including benefits for the heart and brain.

Omega 6 – a type of essential polyunsaturated fat found in sunflower and corn oil. Eating more polyunsaturates is beneficial to health as they help to lower cholesterol and reduce heart disease risk.

Omega 9 – a type of monounsaturated fat found in olive oil and avocado; helps to reduce cholesterol and heart disease risk.

Organosulphur – sulphur-containing compounds in garlic, onions and leeks that have antioxidant and anti-carcinogenic activity in the body.

Oil – a fat that is liquid at room temperature.

Oxalate – compounds found in foods such as rhubarb and spinach that bind to micronutrients such as magnesium and calcium, reducing the bioavailability of these minerals to the body.

P

Papain – enzyme in papaya that is able to break down meat fibre, may have digestive benefits.

Phytochemical (or Phytonutrient) – a general name given to a plant-derived compound that is beneficial to health.

Phytate – a compound in high-fibre foods such as bran and dried pulses that can reduce absorption of nutrients such as calcium, iron and zinc.

Phytonutrient (or Phytochemical) – a general name given to a plant-derived compound that is beneficial to health.

Phytosestrogen – the plant hormone equivalent to animal hormones found in soya products, help reduce circulating blood cholesterol levels.

Phytosterol – a chemical similar to cholesterol that is able to reduce blood cholesterol levels by interfering with absorption in the intestines.

Polyphenol – a compound with antioxidant properties found in foods such as red wine, cocoa and peanuts, thought to reduce heart disease risk.

Polyunsaturate – a type of fat found in sunflower oil, nuts, fish oil and rapeseed oil. A diet high in polyunsaturated fats is known to be beneficial to health.

Proanthocyanidin – a flavonoid, found in cocoa, apples, grapes and red wine, which is a powerful antioxidant and has benefits in heart health, weight management and in preventing cancer.

Probiotics – bacterias such as bifidobacterium and lactobacillus found in bio-yogurts, thought to improve gastrointestinal health.

Protein – made up of amino acids, essential for healthy growth and maintenance of the body.

Proteolytic enzyme – an enzyme that can break down proteins such as papain or bromelain.

Pyridoxine (or vitamin B6) – found in eggs, wholegrains and cruciferous vegetables, essential for making red blood cells and maintaining a healthy immune system.

Q

Quercetin – a flavonoid in tea, red grapes and apples with antioxidant and anti-inflammatory activity, may reduce cancer and heart disease risk.

Quinone – yellow pigment found in spices such as turmeric. Also found in vitamin K, which is essential for blood clotting.

R

RDA (Recommended Dietary Allowance) – the US standard for the amount of a nutrient the average person requires each day to remain healthy.

Resveratrol – a polyphenol found in grapes, red wine and blueberries that has anti-cancer and anti-inflammatory effects.

Retinol – a nutrient that has vitamin A properties and is found in animal foods such as liver, cod liver oil and eggs .

Riboflavin (or vitamin B2) – found in dairy products, pulses and pumpkin seeds. It is essential for energy production and tissue repair.

RNI (Reference Nutrient Intake) – the UK standard for the amount of a nutrient that meets the needs of most healthy people within a group.

Rosmarinic acid – a compound found in rosemary that is high in antioxidants.

S

Shogaol – formed when gingerol in ginger is broken down, has anti-diarrhoea properties.

Sinigrin – a type of glucosinolate in Brussels sprouts and broccoli, may have anti-cancer effects.

Solanine – a toxic compound produced by potatoes when exposed to light.

Soluble fibre – a type of fibre found in oats and pulses that dissolves in water and is partially digested by the body.

Stanol – compound in grains such as amaranth that has blood-cholesterol-reducing activity.

T

Tannin – a polyphenol compound in red wine, pomegranates and berries thought to have antibacterial affects.

Theaflavin – a polyphenol flavonoid in black tea that acts as a powerful antioxidant to protect the body cells from damage by free radicals.

Thearubin – a polyphenol flavonoid, which is a powerful antioxidant, that is found in black tea. It helps to protect body cells from damage by free radicals.

Thiamin (or vitamin B1) – found in wholegrain foods, yeast, pulses and milk and is essential for efficient energy maintenance and muscle growth.

Tocopherol – another name for vitamin E, found in seed oils, eggs, wholegrains and green vegetables; this antioxidant is essential for healthy circulation and skin.

Triglycerides – part of the chemical structure of fats and oils and is made up of three fatty acids. The type of fatty acid found characterizes the type of fat and how it is used by the body.

Tryptophan – an essential amino acid found in poultry, eggs and spirulina, needed for production of the feel-good hormone serotonin and the B-vitamin niacin.

V

Vitamin – a compound needed by the body in very small amounts, for growth and development, and to support metabolism.

W

World Health Organization (WHO) – the co-ordinating body within the United Nations that is responsible for health. The WHO produces policies in the quest to improve public health.

Wholegrain – a food that contains all three parts of the grain, the bran, the germ and endosperm, retaining all its vitamins, minerals and nutrients.

Z

Zeaxanthin – a type of carotenoid yellow pigment found in kale and pumpkins. It is essential for protection of the human eye from damage by free radicals and the development of age-related macular degeneration (ARMD).

Zingerone – formed when gingerone is heated, zingerone is useful in the treatment of diarrhoea.

Index

ACKNOWLEDGEMENTS
Recipes: Catherine Atkinson, Alex Barker, Ghillie Basan, Georgina Campbell, Judith H Dern, Joanna Farrow, Jenni Fleetwood, Brian Glover, Nicola Graimes, Anja Hill, Christine Ingram, Becky Johnson, Bridget Jones, Emi Kazuko, Lucy Knox, Bridget White Lennon, Sara Lewis, Elena Makhonko, Jane Milton, John Nielsen, Maggie Pannell, Carol Pastor, Keith Richmond, Rena Salaman, Ysanne Spevack, Marlena Spieler, Christopher Trotter, Sunil Vijayakar, Jenny White, Kate Whiteman, Carol Wilson, Jeni Wright and Annette Yates.
Photographers: Peter Anderson, Martin Brigdale, Nicky Dowey, Gus Filgate, Amanda Heywood, William Lingwood, Thomas Odulate, Charlie Richards, Craig Robertson, Simon Smith, Jon Whitaker, Mark Wood.